BLOWIN' SMOKE

BLOWIN' SMOKE

*A Trap Shooter's Journey
to the Back Fence and Beyond*

Steve Carmichael

gatekeeper press™
Columbus, Ohio

Blowin' Smoke: A Trap Shooter's Journey to the Back Fence and Beyond

Published by Gatekeeper Press
2167 Stringtown Rd, Suite 109
Columbus, OH 43123-2989
www.GatekeeperPress.com

Library of Congress Control Number: 2021938834

ISBN (hardcover): 9781662913969
ISBN (paperback): 9781662913976
eISBN: 9781662913983

Cover photo www.ByWinslow.com

Original illustrations by Brandy Junod

Dedicated to my family,
and the many friends and acquaintances
met along the way

My sincere thanks to Kenny Ray Estes
Past Director of the ATA Museum and Trapshooting Hall of Fame,
for his dedication to the history of our sport
and assistance with this publication

FOREWORD

I was most pleased when I learned Steve Carmichael was putting together a history of 20th century trap shooting as he was, and is, in a position to write about it that is unique. He writes as both an ATA Hall of Fame competitor and a long-time manager of a large and popular gun club.

Other people have written about trap shooting, mostly about its beginnings and early times. But, the 'Golden Years' as I think of them, was during the period that Steve is writing about in this book. The size of the shoots and the rewards (trophies) are hard to imagine when compared to today's events. How many of you have competed for a new automobile for instance or received an option payoff such as $1400 for a 25 or over $3000 for a 50 straight during a 100-target event? And all this was from shooters entering the options as their fees made up the rewards.

Turn the pages slowly while enjoying this book. There is a lot to be learned as you put yourself into this time frame.

Neal Crausbay, Sweetwater, TX
President, Amateur Trapshooting Association 1995
ATA Trapshooting Hall of Fame Inductee 2007

PROLOGUE

How does one begin a lifetime that's revolved almost exclusively around trapshooting?

I suppose for me it started on a September day in 1959 at the age of 10. My father was reading the sports section of the Sunday "Kansas City Star" newspaper and mentioned an upcoming Ducks Unlimited trapshooting tournament. The event was scheduled the following weekend at Elliott's Shooting Park in Raytown, MO. They were giving away new Winchester Model 12, 20-gauge pump guns to the winner of each class- A, B, C, D, and to the high score in the Hunter's Class. This was exciting news to me as I'd been hunting with him for the prior two years using my Iver Johnson Hercules grade.410 side x side. The little gun was a great starter, but I was eager and ready for an upgrade.

My father, Stanley Howard Carmichael (1926-1992), was raised on a farm in northwest Missouri. He was a survivor, though seriously wounded February 27, 1945, on Iwo Jima with the 3rd Marine Division. He was barely nineteen years old. He was designated as a light machine gunner and carried the Browning Automatic Rifle, better known as the BAR. His wounds were from mortar shrapnel accompanied by blast concussion on the black sand of the beach.

Just prior to the mortar attack, his platoon was strafed by machine gun fire that ripped his canteen and extra ammo pouches off both sides of his web belt, somehow missing his entire body mass. Two thirds of the men that accompanied him that day were not as fortunate.

Today's youth truly have no concept of that kind of hell.

It's only by sheer luck that I'm here to tell the story and share the photo below. While a man of few words, he embraced strong family values and led by an example I've aspired to duplicate my entire life. He was the best.

Stanley Howard Carmichael (right)
Recovering on Guam, April 1945

Dad was an excellent wing shot but had never attempted anything more formal than a few clays from a hand thrower. I can honestly say I had never seen him miss anything he had shot at, with shotgun, handgun, or large caliber rifle. Ever.

The following week we made the drive across town to the shooting park. He went into the clubhouse and signed up. A long-time fixture of Elliott's Shooting Park, Jack Thompson, was at the handicap table and asked the usual questions about his past trapshooting experience. Dad said "none" on a regulation trap field, but admitted he was an excellent shot with rifle, pistol, or shotgun. Jack immediately placed him in the Hunter's Class and asked him to listen for his name to be called over the PA, announcing when and where his squad would be shooting.

As this was a 50-bird event, two boxes of shells were purchased. Federal Monarks with the image of the clay target breaking on the box if I recall. We returned to the car and he removed his only shotgun from the soft case in the trunk; a hump-back Browning 3" Auto 5 with plain 32" barrel. This was his duck, goose, pheasant, and quail gun. I had seen it many times and could attest that he was deadly with it.

Eventually, we heard his name called and made our way to the starting trap. I sat on a bench and found a pencil and a piece of cardboard I used for keeping score.

One thing I noticed as he started shooting was that he had to eject each spent round by manually pulling the bolt back. He was also deliberate, riding each target almost to its crest. But he appeared to be doing OK.

As trap targets do, they were going right, left, and all over, but that didn't seem to affect him. At the end of the first round of 25 targets,

I had nothing but "X" on my box lid. Same for the second 25. Sure enough, he had broken all 50 targets.

He put his gun away and we returned to the clubhouse amidst quite a stir. Mr. Thompson pulled dad aside and stated that anyone in the Hunter's Class should not be breaking 50 straight and offered him the opportunity to try again in a different class.

My father was easy-going, but I could tell this really got under his skin. We left, feeling somewhat cheated and with a bit of a bad taste in our mouth. However, a seed had been planted and he discovered trapshooting was a game he had the natural talent to excel at.

By the following Spring he had purchased a field grade Winchester Model 12, then added a Simmons ventilated rib. He made his own Monte Carlo trap stock in my uncle's basement. A year later, he placed 4th in the Grand American Handicap in Vandalia, OH. Two years following that, he won the car at Elliott's annual flagship event; the MOKAN Handicap. It appeared if any redemption was due, it had been achieved.

At one of the Elliott's tournaments in 1961 or 1962, we pulled in early one morning and discovered a small tent had been erected in the grassy portion of the parking lot. Under the canopy sat a single occupant by the name of Larry Roe. Dad was carrying his Model 12 as we approached the tent. Mr. Roe took the opportunity to extend his hand and introduce himself, and said he was an engraver. He also had a severe case of the shakes.

Mr. Roe said for $12 he would engrave both sides of the gun's receiver in the hope of stimulating business as the shooting crowd arrived. He had photos on the table of some of his previous work which was quite impressive. Reluctantly my Dad agreed and was told to come back in one hour. At this point, Mr. Roe pulled out a pint bottle of something, took a couple of swigs, then sat down to do the work. He now appeared totally calm and collected, ready to tackle the tedious work.

When we returned, we found the gun had been engraved perfectly and people standing all around watching the engraver in awe. Three or four guns were tagged and now laying on the table waiting for their turn.

We heard later this same gentleman had engraved the Lord's Prayer on the head of a straight pin seven different times. I've never been able to confirm this but one of the pins supposedly was given to Independence, Missouri resident, and past President of the United States, Harry Truman.

I formally ventured into the trapshooting game following the 1961 Grand American as I received a new Model 12 trap gun from Simmons Gun Shop in downtown Kansas City shortly thereafter. I began registering targets in 1962 and started earning a few Sub-Junior, then Junior trophies along the way. Dad and I paired to win the Father & Son Championship on Monday at the 1966 Grand American. Two days later I won the Junior Clay Target Championship.

It was also during the 1966 Grand that I met Major Tom Gilmore for the first time. The Major was head of the moving target section and a recruiter for the U.S. Army Marksmanship Training Unit at Ft. Benning, GA.

The Major inquired about my future as I still had a year of high school remaining. I mentioned college was in the picture. He said he would like for me to consider coming to Ft. Benning if interested in the shooting program. I would be asked to enlist in the U.S. Army for a three-year stint. Following Basic Training, I would report directly to the Marksmanship Training Unit, and could expect to stay there for the entire three years if I made the team. He also mentioned the unit was due to receive approximately one million dollars each year for 1968, 1969 and 1970 to cover expenses associated with extensive European travel and competition.

I returned home and entered my senior year of high school that fall, but my conversation with the Major often occupied my thoughts.

After graduation the following spring, and three months of summer work, I enlisted in the United States Army on October 23, 1967. As an only child this decision followed several lengthy discussions with my concerned parents. College would have to wait. I completed eight weeks of Basic Training at Ft. Leonard Wood, MO, then proceeded directly to Ft. Benning.

The shooting program at that time consisted of a 90-day, temporary duty (TDY) tryout period. The incentive to make the team was ever-present as the Vietnam war was at its peak in Southeast Asia. Many of the non-commissioned officers at the Marksmanship Training Unit were assigned an Infantry MOS, or Military Occupational Specialty. Not making the team could certainly result in eight weeks at Ft. Polk, LA, for Small Arms Infantry Training, then directly to South Vietnam. Fortunately, I excelled quickly at the International Trap game and made the European travelling team the first year. Former Junior acquaintances Gene Lumsden (CA) and Eddie Leavendusky (KS) were both on the team, as were Jim Beck (NE), Ron Lucas (IL), Rusty Anderson (KS) and Steve Thoele (MN). Ray Stafford (CO), Doug Elson (OH), Mike Cleary (MI), Glen Everts (WI), and Dallas Krapf (PA) were the other rookies on the trap team during this period.

A typical Monday-Friday consisted of 50 practice targets in the morning, lunch break, then 50 more in the afternoon. By today's standards, that doesn't sound like a lot of shooting, but you must consider popular International Trap ammunition at that time consisted of 3 ¼ dram, 1 ¼ of shot. Recoil certainly played a role. Some afternoons included optional second barrel practice sessions. We often handloaded our own shells with size #11 or #12 shot. These would be used in our first barrel to assure there would be a large piece or whole target remaining following the first shot. This made for excellent second-barrel practice. International Trap requires you learn very quickly that the second shot must be made immediately when needed or will be ineffective.

While competing in the United States, many days were spent on the road travelling, two per car, between tournaments. One stretch in the fall of 1969 took us all the way from Montreal, Canada, to Renton, WA.

For each of the following three years, 1968, 1969 and 1970, six to eight weeks were spent in Europe participating in Grand Prix Tournaments. Competitions took us to Italy, Switzerland, Austria, Germany, Denmark, Romania, Czechoslovakia, and Belgium. We we're part of an elite group serving as ambassadors of the sport and were undefeated in domestic and World International Trap team competitions over the 3-year period. Our average age was about 21, and we were competing against Europe's most established and experienced national teams.

It was a great time in my life, and I was extremely fortunate to have such an experience. My military days had been the extreme opposite of the brutal nightmare my father had endured in the Pacific. I left Ft. Benning for the last time September 1, 1970, and, as I had promised my parents, began college within a week.

Trapshooting competitions while in college were few and far between, but I made it to a couple of state tournaments and a couple of Grand Americans during this period. I was fortunate that the ACUI Collegiate Championships were right in my back yard at the Missouri Trapshooter's Association home grounds at Linn Creek in 1971 and 1972. I managed to garner a couple of individual collegiate titles along with team wins for the University of Missouri.

In the spring of 1973, I acquired my first Perazzi Comp 1 Single, later designated as the TM1, brand new, for $600. It was serial #286 if I remember correctly. The early models were fitted with a big round forearm and an extremely thick-walled barrel at the muzzle. In my opinion, the arrival of the TM1 did more for long-yardage shooters in the ATA than anything that preceded it. The hyper-fast lock time of the trigger, overall balance, and natural pointing ability were unlike anything else on the market. My handicap scores improved immediately. Within a month I captured the All-Around Championship at the Missouri State Shoot.

At the 1973 Grand American, I received the high 27-yard award with a 96 in the Grand American Handicap. This would be unheard of these days, but back then, a coveted Steiff-engraved, sterling silver bowl was awarded to the high score posted from each yard. Can you imagine, a 96 winning anything today in the Grand American Handicap?

I returned to the Grand in 1974, ending as runner-up to Hiram Bradley in the Singles Championship and managed to win the Doubles and All-Around Championships. I was presented with a very special memorial award from the parents of the late James P. Defilippi Jr. Jimmy was the youngest person ever to win the Grand American Doubles Championship at the age of 16 in 1963. This award has always occupied a prominent place in my home.

Following graduation from the University of Missouri in the spring of 1975, I spent the next seven years attending trapshooting tournaments around the United States. This was not according to plan, but one tournament led to the next, and then another. My original intent upon receiving my biology degree was to be enrolled in veterinary school by the fall of 1975.

I soon drifted far away from that.

Trapshooting tournaments that first summer led to tournaments in the fall, and additional tournaments the following spring. Tournaments were financially lucrative during this period, plus provided exposure to a variety of business opportunities. Along my journey I was involved in industry-related product design, development & endorsement for Reinhart Fajen, Action Products and Benson Optical. I conducted clinics and individual instruction through-out the United States and was selected to be a member of the first Winchester/Western Ammunition Advisory Group.

This early period was a great time in my life and paved the way for everything that was to follow. This also confirmed my belief in the possibility of a pre-ordained destiny, and that we all may be pawns on a massive game board of life.

So be it, I was along for the ride, though it would be bumpy at times.

The title of this book was derived from an unfortunate incident that occurred during a major handicap at the Grand American in Vandalia, Ohio over forty years ago.

There was a time in my trapshooting career that I was in the habit of chewing gum while shooting. I wasn't especially fond of chewing gum; I think I just did it now and then such as a baseball player uses chewing tobacco or sunflower seeds. Something to keep you occupied between shots.

I was only down one target in the first 60-some of the event and would occasionally blow the smoke out of the barrel and chamber area following my shot. Anyone that used the paper Winchester Super Target load of the late 1970s would remember the acrid smoke that sometimes trailed a freshly ejected hull. This extremely offensive byproduct was right on the edge of being classified in the same category as tear gas. Combined with a calm, hot, and humid day could lead to a coughing and choking fit in the middle of a round.

Attempting to disperse the smoke, I blew the gum right down the barrel of the TM1 and it stuck inside towards the muzzle end. I proceeded to gently shake it while trying not to distract my fellow squad members. It finally dislodged just as it was my turn to shoot again, now totally out of rhythm with myself. "Lost", then another "lost" shortly after. I ended with a 97. The payoff difference between 97, 98 and 99 in a major handicap event was immense in those days. I've since refrained from chewing gum while shooting.

I've made every attempt to chronicle the places and the people I've interacted with along the way accurately, and to the best of my recollection. Regrettably, most of the places mentioned, and a good portion of the people, are no longer with us. However, the memories remain with me.

I'm quite certain many of you close to my age are likely to find something in the following pages you can relate to. For those younger and newer to the game, this may provide you with a sense of how it used to be.

I hope you enjoy reading this compilation as much as I've enjoyed placing it on paper. It has provided me an opportunity to re-visit and savor many fond moments of days long past.

Contents

PLACES MOSTLY FORGOTTEN

THE GOLDEN WEST GRAND (GWG)

Formerly the Jabberwock Gun Club, then purchased by the Smith family in 1950, Harold's Trapshooting Country Club would become home to the Golden West Grand in 1952; the first major trapshooting tournament in the western United States. Harold S. Smith developed, promoted, and hosted the tournament during its heyday, and was second only to the Grand American in attendance, monies, and prizes. This was the first location west of the Mississippi River to host over a thousand trap shooters in a single event. Mr. Smith also introduced one of the most coveted prizes in trapshooting, the gold coin belt buckle.

Upon opening, the facility included 12 trap fields, eight skeet fields and two flyer fields. A great promoter, Harold's Club in downtown Reno was promoted around the world. At one time over 2000 signs lined major highways throughout the world, featuring the red and black Conestoga wagons bearing the declaration "Harold's Club or Bust".

I looked forward to going to Reno at every opportunity and attended several Golden West Grand tournaments at this location during the late 1970s and 1980s. Shooting conditions could be wonderful or awful, but at some time during the week you could always count on a few challenging days of weather.

The old clubhouse was a late 1940s, early 1950s classic, and represented Harold's Club and Reno in the old western tradition exactly as you would expect. There were ample tables and seating area for guests, a huge L-shaped bar that dominated the entire main open area, and a locker room that was entirely too small! The entire place reeked of an abundance of character.

Near the west entrance, a wall-mounted display case contained Arnold Riegger's Winchester Model 37 and Model 12 trap guns, both with several layers of cardboard taped to the combs of the buttstocks to raise the height. I have no idea if Arnold was just trying to improve his view over the receiver, or this was an effort to raise the point of impact for each of the guns. This was long before adjustable combs were available, now standard features on almost all modern tournament grade shotguns.

At the tournament registration area during many Reno tournaments, you could expect to find Norm Volponi heading up the cashiering team and Hilda Fleming in charge of placing shooters on squads. Norm was a superb numbers and people-person; Hilda was excellent, but firm.

Texas shooter Troy Collier was fresh out of the Junior ranks when he made his first trip to Reno. He meandered through the long line in the sign-up process and was finally standing in front of Hilda. She was working with several large master squad sheets that faced towards her and away from Troy. Hilda was manually entering names and yardages with a pencil equipped with an eraser. (Trap shooters were notorious for changing squads and positions; still are for that matter. This was many years before the luxury of computer programs, and everything was done by hand).

Troy was cranking his neck around to see the squad sheets, trying to find a starting position he liked, preferably on a squad with someone he recognized. Hilda recommended two or three open spots which Troy refused. This went back and forth for several minutes. Those waiting in line were becoming impatient. Finally, Troy said "Uh, excuse me Ma'am, but I don't shoot with just anybody," with which Hilda responded "Well sonny, then it appears you won't be shooting at all. Next in line please."

Trapshooting was derived directly from live pigeon shooting events that started in Europe many years ago, eventually coming to the United States. In live pigeons, or clays on a trap field, money wagers have historically been part of both games to provide contestants the opportunity of financial return for a good score. In a 100-target trapshooting event, traditionally you could wager on each 25, on the first and last 50, and the total 100. Other optional variations included the Lewis Class which added an element of luck. Wagering was extremely popular, probably more so in the early days of trapshooting than it has been in recent years.

Norm and his excellent crew figured all optional entries and payoffs by hand. When you considered multiple events often exceeding 500 shooters, and each contestant may enter a variety of options, this was no meager task. Norm was recognized as an excellent cashier of trapshooting tournaments, providing both speed and accuracy. Usually, within an hour or two of an event's completion, all payoffs were posted. Norm was a valuable fixture of major programs in the western states for many years.

The trap houses at the old Reno grounds were less than perfect as the straightaway target appeared about 18" to the right of where it should have been. Whomever had built the concrete trap pedestals overlooked the necessary offset required for the venerable handset Western V1524 machines.

As a competitor, you had to adjust to the offset straightaway quickly on each visit as this was the only trap club that I ever experienced this. The trap fields themselves were not all facing quite true north. Once you crossed the canal heading east, the line turned slightly towards the northeast. Everyone walked the full length of the firing line during a 100-target event; the shooting of 4-trap banks was unheard of. If you wanted to tune-up prior to an event, the lone practice field was on the edge of the parking lot facing straight south.

With all its beloved flaws, most were overlooked due to the strong optional and purse participation creating huge payouts. I once missed my 99th target in the feature handicap costing me the back 50-straight, resulting in a total of 96 instead of 97. That turned out to be a $7,000 target. The visibility and overall conditions were difficult that day but very typical of Reno in early May.

In 1979, our GWG squad consisted of Dan Orlich, Dan Bonillas, me, and John Hall. I can't recall who was shooting the number 5 position with us that year. That weekend we endured some of the strongest winds I can ever remember competing in as gusts up to 60 mph were recorded. The Doubles Championship was Saturday morning with winds from behind and target pairs diving into the ground. Only six scores were recorded that made it into the 90s with Bonillas having the field-high score of 93. Kevin Alexander, Pat Moore, and Leo Harrison III with 92s, Kay Ohye with 91, Brad Dysinger with 90; that was it. John Hall had an 87 and I squeaked out an 88. Dan B also won the Preliminary Handicap that afternoon with 94, after a tie and shoot-off.

Sunday's weather worsened, as temperatures plummeted and winds shifted from the north, but Bonillas went on to win the Handicap Championship with a lone 95. This was a tremendous weekend performance in these conditions.

The GWG experienced ups and downs in the early 1980s but flourished during the mid-1980s while under the guidance of Pat Moore. The facility became known just as "The Gun Club" at this time. It was still at its original location on Pyramid Way northeast of downtown Reno. The last GWG held there in 1989 had an attendance of over 1000 shooters. It may have continued successfully at this location for many years if not for the actions of an ATA Executive Committee Member. At this time, the ATA controlled the naming rights to any tournament using the name "Grand". The Executive in question didn't approve of the way the GWG was progressing and could not persuade Mr. Moore to see things his way. He finally decided to award the 1990 tournament to the new Sage Hill Clay Sports facility which was still under construction south of Reno. This change took place just after Pat Moore had renewed his lease but could no longer justify keeping the grounds with the loss of the flagship event. The historic property was vacated, much to the sorrow of a multitude of past trapshooting guests and supporters.

The 1990 GWG moved to Sage Hill as planned, hosting over 1300 total shooters their first year, with over 400 entering the events held on the opening Monday. Trap & Field magazine continued to promote the junket and flights out of Indianapolis and Chicago as they had for many years. Senior Editor Joan Davis was there to cover the events. Unfortunately, this trend did not continue. When the GWG returned to Sage Hill in 1991 attendance had dropped considerably. The total number of shooters for the week fell to 750. Joan Davis, Trap & Field, the junket, and almost half the shooters were gone in a single year. Eventually, the traditional compulsory purses were eliminated for the final two handicap events. The GWG continued to lose popularity, eventually becoming a weekend event before the Sage Hill facility closed its doors in November 2013.

In May of 2014, a dedicated group of western shooters, combined with the directors of the Livermore Pleasanton Rod & Gun Club, held the GWG in California for the first time. Dan Orlich even made the trip to the new location to welcome all attendees to the new site.

The GWG has continued at Livermore to this day, keeping this grand old tournament alive hosting 150-200 shooters annually.

I believe I may have fired at the very last competition target at the original Harold's Club location during the 1989 Golden West Grand. It was the All-Around shoot-off with Ray Stafford and Dan Bonillas. I ended up with the win after two consecutive 40X40 rounds.

After completing the shoot-off, I cased up the guns, closed the trunk and drove away. I was quite aware this would likely be my last visit to this historic trapshooting property.

LITTLE MONDEAUX GUN CLUB

Not long after the move of the Golden West Grand from The Gun Club to the Sage Hill Clay Sports facility, rumors began circulating of another major trapshooting facility being constructed in the general vicinity of Carson City. The rumors proved to be true.

In the fall of 1990, Tombstone Pizza co-founder, Ron Simek, opened the Little Mondeaux Lodge & Gun Club on Jacks Valley Road overlooking Carson Valley. After selling Tombstone Pizza to the Kraft Corporation in 1986 for a staggering $386,000,000, Simek purchased the ranch previously owned by Harvey Gross of Harvey's Resort Hotel & Casino at Lake Tahoe. A lodge complete with restaurant and bar, plus a 32-trap layout were constructed making this one of the largest trap clubs west of the Mississippi at that time. And, within 40 miles of the Sage Hill facility, new home of the Golden West Grand.

Plans materialized quickly to bring a major trapshooting event to the new facility. In April 1991, Simek introduced the First Annual Sierra Grand Trapshooting Tournament featuring $25,000 in trophies and $25,000 in added money, just two weeks prior to the Golden West Grand at Sage Hill. Harvey's Resort co-sponsored the event.

In 1992, this facility hosted the Second Annual Sierra Grand in April, the Nevada State Trapshooting Championships in June, and the ATA Western Zone Tournament in July.

I attended all the events mentioned above and had the opportunity to become well acquainted with Mr. Simek. He obviously had a considerable investment in Little Mondeaux and it certainly piqued my interest. I discovered he was also eager to pick my mind. We met for a long dinner one evening at the lodge during the 1992 Nevada State Shoot.

We shared a tremendous amount of conversation about the trapshooting world and several interesting things were revealed. The attendance of the two events that Little Mondeaux had hosted up to that point in 1992 had been about what I had expected, nothing huge or small, just typical. This was also true for the first Sierra Grand in 1991.

Finally, I just asked what had been on my mind- "Ron, whatever possessed you to build such a place as this?" He responded- "I was told if I built such a facility, I could have a tournament every month that would draw over a thousand shooters each."

I was obviously surprised by this- "Who on earth told you that?"

"Jack" he answered.

"Jack DeMars?" I asked.

"Yes."

Jack DeMars had been his manager at Little Mondeaux since opening.

For the previous 20 years I had attended about every major trapshooting tournament in the West and Southwest and had an extreme amount of difficulty understanding how such a prediction could be justified.

Ron went on- "When I put the numbers to it, it looked pretty good!" I explained to him there were only about three tournaments in the western half of the United States that had any history or capability of drawing 1000 shooters. One, the Golden West Grand of the old days, two, the Spring Grand in Arizona, and three, the California State Shoot. That was it, no more. He said- "Boy, I wish I would have talked to you before I did this!"

For those that never saw this facility, it was first-class all the way. The 32 fields were amply spaced, overladen with fresh sod sprouting green grass, and new scoring stands, tables and gun racks on each field. The view was spectacular with the Carson Valley laying out before you. A special outdoor camera had been installed to view the on-deck squad board allowing images to be broadcast to monitors inside the building and RVs that were on the property. The lodge was not just a clubhouse, but rather an upscale restaurant and bar. However, downstairs provided ample room for classification and squad personnel, plus plenty of room for cashiers for conducting large tournaments.

Shooting on the fields could be interesting at times. For one thing, they faced east-northeast so early squads best be avoided or you'd have the sun peaking in under the bill of your cap. You could also experience very strong winds.

During the final handicap of the 1992 Nevada State Shoot was such a time.

It was Father's Day, Sunday, June 14, and eight inches of fresh snow had fallen overnight on the Sierra's surrounding Lake Tahoe immediately to the West. Though it wasn't snowing at Little Mondeaux, snowflakes were blowing through the air for most of the handicap, riding the winds down the mountainside.

On another occasion, we encountered strong tail winds coming off the mountain during a doubles event. It was fortunate the ground dropped dramatically in front of the trap house as I witnessed many second targets of the pairs being broken four to six feet below the grade of the shooting stations.

While plans included a large premium RV park with full hook-ups, a critical error had been discovered. Due to the location and grade of the chosen RV area, installation of a septic system would not be allowed. This would have been in violation of some health code regarding the location of the restaurant. Ron had ordered dozens of custom RV pedestals that would never be used.

So, after the 1992 season, Ron Simek decided this was a venture that was not going to deliver for him. Attendance was not even close to projections. After only two years of operation, the Little Mondeaux Gun Club ceased operations. In the Spring of 1993, I took advantage of the liquidation sale, purchasing all the scoring stands, gun racks, and the closed-circuit camera set-up. These would all be put to good use at the Las Vegas Gun Club.

Bing Crosby's widow, Kathryn, lived just north of the facility and opposed its construction from the very beginning. I'm not sure if that played any role in its demise or not.

Not long after the closure, I heard Ron made a deal with the existing golf course located south of the facility. They would benefit from the lodge and expand the course to the north. Financially, I have a feeling he made out very well. He struck me as one of those unique individuals who seem to possess the rare ability to turn a potentially bad financial situation into a good one with little effort. I encourage everyone to research Ron Simek and his brother's amazing story in the development of Tombstone Pizza and how he came to be in the Carson Valley.

This must have been some type of record for a facility of this magnitude to appear, then disappear, just like that.

BOB TAYLOR'S TRAPSHOOTING COUNTRY CLUB

Bob Taylor's "Ranch House Supper Club" was well-known by Las Vegas locals long before being discovered by tournament trap shooters. Founded in 1955, aged sides of beef, exclusively from Chicago Stockyard Packing were delivered weekly and placed in a large walk-in cooler. Bob took it from there, making each cut exactly as he wanted it. For years, Bob personally cooked every steak on heavy steel grates over an open mesquite coal fire in the main room of the restaurant. He was very meticulous about this, using only plain white paper to start the fire, and never any type of starting fluid. Steaks were tested for degrees of doneness by touch in the dim light.

The restaurant itself was cozy and felt exactly like what it was commonly referred to- a supper house. You entered through a small single door and progressed through a narrow hallway. A collection of rare Jim Beam collector's decanters on display occupying lighted glass shelves to your right.

The small bar area was cozy and looked like a mini western saloon. Signed photos of celebrities adorned the natural wood paneled walls. A hostess greeted you at this point and escorted you to your table where you would enjoy one of the finest meals you've ever experienced.

To bring notoriety to the restaurant in its early days, Bob travelled to a livestock show in Chicago and purchased a Grand Champion Bull by the name of Herkie. An Associated Press photo appeared in newspapers throughout the U.S. depicting Bob, dressed in his most fashionable western wear, making the purchase of Herkie with a wheelbarrow full of silver dollars. A special outdoor pen was built for Herkie between the parking lot and entry into the restaurant and he became a talking point and favorite of those frequenting the property. Unfortunately, Bob received a phone call one morning from one of the caretakers that he needed to get over to the restaurant immediately. Something had happened to his prized bull. Sure enough, Bob arrived to find Herkie deceased, lying in the pen. Facing a potential marketing nightmare, a backhoe was hastily located and Herkie was removed before the evening crowd started to arrive. To make matters worse, it was soon discovered the lucrative insurance policy on the prize bull had expired by three days.

Bob had a love of shooting clay targets and constructed three trap and skeet fields on the east side of the restaurant. Ann Margaret and Elvis Presley's skeet shooting scene was filmed at this location during the making of "Viva Las Vegas." When Ann was filmed shooting, it was Bob breaking the targets just out of sight of the camera.

Over the years, Bob delved further and further into the clay target shooting business, opening a proper clubhouse and small pro shop on the south side of the restaurant.

Additional trap fields were added, 20 in all, going to the East and facing straight north. Bob was soon promoting many new trapshooting events, often providing multiple automobiles as prizes and featuring some of the largest cash purses in history.

Bob also employed some of the most impressive dining room staff I've encountered in my years of travel.

During a winter tournament in 1976, a group of eight of us decided to dine at the Ranch House following the day's events. Our waiter that evening was a tall distinguished looking black gentleman dressed very professionally in white shirt, black vest, and black slacks. There was an array of complex orders taken for our group. Ribeye rare, New York medium rare, prime rib, shrimp cocktails, etc., plus a variety of beverages. As our waiter was taking the second order, I noticed he was not writing anything down. This was also noticed by another member of our group and we traded glances. Finally, one of us asked "Shouldn't you be writing this down?" At this point he just smiled and said "No, I've got this." After he had taken all eight orders and departed, bets were being placed on who would receive what correctly. To our absolute amazement, everyone received exactly what they had ordered. I remember discussions about this for many months to follow.

It was during this same time that many visiting trap shooters stayed downtown at the Mint or Golden Nugget hotel. Downtown Las Vegas was a fun place back in these days with so many different hotels and casinos within easy walking distance.

One evening I ventured across the street to the Golden Nugget. After entering, I could see a large group of people up ahead, standing just outside a small lounge on the left side of the room A ballad was being sung and could easily be heard pouring out of the lounge, accompanied only by a piano and acoustic guitar.

I recognized a shooter in the overflow crowd and asked what was going on. He said there's a singer in there named Willie Nelson, and his sister was on the piano.

Sure enough, Willie was in there singing songs from his newly released "Red-Headed Stranger" album, and within weeks of achieving super stardom. I purchased the album shortly after and listened to it over-and-over again while driving across America's highways that year.

There was an NFL-Pro Am trapshooting tournament in 1977, featuring 26 NFL players such as Carl Eller, Robert Newhouse, Tom Dempsey, Don Nottingham & Ed Flanagan. Other events included the "100 Grand", the "50 Grand", and eventually the "250 Grand (or Super Shoot)" in 1985, which featured $100,000 in added money from the Landmark Hotel & Casino.

By the time the Super Shoot rolled around, Bob had sold the Ranch House property, though it still carried is name. Bob approached Gary Williams who was managing the Mint Gun Club at that time. This was a neighboring facility with 24 trap fields four miles to the NW of the Ranch House. An agreement was signed, and the Super Shoot was on.

This was an extremely attractive program and though I hadn't competed for months due to my Alaska residency, decided this would be well worth making the effort. In desperate need of practice, I flew to Arizona early, allowing time for a few days to tune-up and compete in Phoenix just prior to the Las Vegas program.

Bonillas and I shot several events together at the Phoenix Trap & Skeet Club, but Dan left Friday afternoon to be in Las Vegas when registration opened at noon the next day. There was quite a buzz about the Las Vegas tournament, and it appeared there would be a tremendous crowd. He felt it was important to secure our squads as the program would begin the following Monday. I continued to stay in Phoenix for the weekend trying to get as many targets under my belt as possible before heading to Las Vegas.

The Super Shoot was to be the first computerized trapshooting tournament. Bob had hired a young computer-savvy gent to set everything up. There was to be a very small support staff to assist with cashiering, composed only of Norm & Jane Volponi. Norm was apprehensive as a large crowd was expected to attend. There was no pre-squad and no proven track records for computerized shoots prior to this time. Nobody knew what to expect.

I was lying in bed watching TV in the Phoenix motel room Saturday evening when my phone rang at about 10pm. There was no "Hello" or anything else coming over the phone, just "You owe me big". Dan was on the other end and proceeded to tell me of the day's events. He had arrived at the club early enough Saturday to be fourth in line for registration. Four hours later he'd achieved his mission of obtaining our squads.

When sign-up began, the first person in line approached the computer whiz at the cashier's window, provided him with the events and options he had selected and proceeded to pay. All good, then he was assigned squad 1, post 1. The next person in line now comes forward, goes through the same process, and was assigned squad 1, post 2. A major setback was revealed at this point; nothing in the computer program had allowed for the possibility of incompatible yardages. The complete computer operation was immediately scrapped, and everything would have to be accomplished by hand; with a staff of two. It was at this point that chaos set in as many attendees had already showed up for registration.

Monday arrived and the first day of the event came off without any noticeable problems. Cool and breezy, but nothing like what was about to come. Tuesday the weather deteriorated with temperatures dropping and wind increasing. Wednesday & Thursday were two of the most difficult days I've ever encountered on a trap field. Plus, there were two handicaps each day. Temperatures were in the low 30s and wind out of the northwest 30-40mph. The all black targets looked like tiny aspirins. This is the only time in my shooting career I can remember breaking four scores in a row in the mid to upper 70s. You just hoped you could break 4 on a post as 5 was almost unheard of.

On the third field of one of these miserable events, I struggled to finish with a score of 13. While checking the final scores, Bonillas looked over at me and said- "Damn Carmichael, don't believe I've every broken a 13!" I mumbled something to the fact that I hadn't either up to that point. We moved on to our fourth trap.

About halfway through the last round it dawned on me that Dan was taking a tremendous amount of losses. The cold wind in our face was still howling. We're finally on our last post. Dan missed the first four out, and I remember thinking; I could only recall a single time that someone had a zero on a post while on our squad. It finally comes around to his last target. He drew a high left and didn't shoot. Starts over, re-mounts, calls, drew another high left and didn't shoot again. Bad pulls? Possibly, the wind was howling making it difficult for the puller to hear. I knew from past experience that high, climbing left angles from post 1 were Dan's Achilles Heel. At this point we all look over at him and he says something like "f _ _ _ you guys, if you want to take it away from me go ahead." Under the circumstances, we didn't. He finally drew a straightaway and broke it in half for "1" on the last post.

After the round we gathered around the scorekeeper for final scores. I couldn't help myself, and finally said- "Damn Bonillas, I don't believe I've ever broken a 12, and it should have been an 11!" He responded with another "f _ _ _ you" and left the field. Don Slavich (CA) witnessed the entire fiasco. He was supposed to be on our squad. Instead he was sitting in his Cadillac with the heater on, obviously amused by our inadequate efforts he had just observed.

As expected, a high number of shooters turned out for the tournament, but, due to the nasty weather conditions, were leaving at about the same rate they were arriving. Over 950 individuals were handicapped during the week, but the largest entry of a single event was Saturday's handicap with 674. Events through Thursday barely exceeded 300 entries. It was an extremely difficult week for Bob Taylor, following a tremendous amount of investment, facility improvements, and planning.

The $100,000 in added money from the Landmark Hotel & Casino was to be given away to the top 10 finishers as follows. There was a total of ten handicaps over the seven-day period. There were two yardage groups; 19-23.5, and 24-27. If you tied for high or runner-up in your yardage group in any of the ten events, you qualified for a fifty-target shoot-off Sunday afternoon following the final handicap event. The top ten scores after fifty targets would shoot another 25 targets to determine final placement. Winner of the shoot-off received $50,000 and substantial cash payoffs continued down for the remainder of the top ten finalists.

Friday's handicap carried over into Saturday, and Saturday's handicap was destined to carry over into Sunday. It was obvious to me the final shoot-off Sunday afternoon would have to be held in the dark. I found Bob at the end of the bar following Friday's events and asked if he had any white targets on the grounds (we were shooting all black during the week). Another load of targets was being delivered Saturday and it made sense to throw a few cases of white targets in. At this time, the old club had only two poorly lit fields, so even white would not be great. Bob said- "No problem, we won't need them, we'll be done plenty early on Sunday." Indeed, a large portion of Saturdays' handicap carried over into Sunday. The final event, and subsequent shoot-offs, were destined to start very late.

The sun sets early in Las Vegas during the month of January. By 4:30pm, it's long beyond the mountain peaks to the west.

Sure enough, the last handicap event ran late, plus they had to determine the qualifiers from the last event before any final shoot-offs could be held.

The first round of shoot-offs for the $100,000 were called to the line around 3:45, on all black targets. Everyone would shoot two rounds for a total of 50 targets each. If I remember correctly, the results were three scores of 47, and eleven scores of 46 to establish the top ten. These fourteen shooters would participate in an additional 25 target round shoot-off to determine the top ten. No chance, it was now completely dark, and shooting was out of the question. Bob asked if everyone could come back Monday but that was impossible for many due to travel plans. One of the finalists had a flight to Honolulu that evening; another was scheduled for an I.R.S. audit the next day. Bob desperately needed a photo of someone holding the large wooden check for $50,000. The group decided the $82,000 designated for the top 12 would be split evenly fourteen ways. Those that could come out the next day and shoot for the photo with the check would do so. If I remember correctly, Daro Handy was amongst those returning Monday and appeared in the photo. As luck would have it, the weather was perfect on Monday.

The Super Shoot was a financial disaster, and not just for Bob. He had a total of 5 investors backing necessary club improvements and the program itself. The total loss was tremendous. One of the investors denied his financial obligation and Bob was left holding the bag. All payouts could not be made from the last event and would eventually result in Bob Taylor being banned for life from the ATA.

I sat with Bob at the Awards Dinner Sunday night following completion of the Super Shoot. This was held at the top of the Landmark. I'm sure Bob was in no mood for festivity but remained gracious to the very end. During the evening, A PA announcement came over the speakers "Telephone call for Bob Taylor." He really didn't feel like talking to anyone at that point. He turned to his partner, Dotti, and asked if she would take the call. She was gone for a few minutes, then returned all bouncy & bubbly and announced- "The jackets just arrived!" Bob had ordered dozens of high-quality jackets with "Super Shoot" on the sleeves. These were patterned after Porsche racing team jackets and would have been terrific sellers the week of the tournament. He looked at me, shrugged, and simply said "Perfect ending."

Regardless of what may be said about Bob Taylor now or in the future, I knew him only as a great promoter of trapshooting. He never stopped trying to achieve a better tournament that offered shooters something memorable and truly substantial to compete for.

Bob and I, along with Wayne Leslie (CO), Charlie Sheckler (PA), and Phil & Judy Matthews (MO) floated the Karluk River on Kodiak Island in June of 1978. After a long day on the river, Bob cooked steaks one evening over an open fire in the dark, perfectly done, by touch. Nothing ever tasted better.

The heavy grates from his outdoor grill at the Ranch House ended up in the outdoor grill at the Las Vegas Gun Club, and finally part of the grill in my backyard.

Bob passed away in 2010, one day short of his 88th birthday. I was honored to speak at his services. A true Las Vegas icon was gone, but the steakhouse still carries his name today.

THE MISSOURI FALL HANDICAP

Located in the heart of the Ozarks, the Missouri Fall Handicap was one of the premier money trapshooting events of the last three decades of the twentieth century. The property, facility, and funds to maintain this venue were donated by long-time Missouri shooter W.F. Fienup. This would become home of the Missouri Trapshooter's Association and expanded to a total of 60 trap fields as the Fall Handicap crowd grew to burgeoning proportions. The Missouri State Championships were held earlier in the year during the month of May but drew about half the attendance of the fall tournament. Close to the Lake of the Ozarks with numerous accommodations and restaurants, the Missouri Fall Handicap was an annual must-attend for hundreds of shooters. Area lodging in Osage Beach would be dominated by trap shooters the week of the event, many with bass boats in tow. Restaurants such as the Potted Steer and Blue Heron welcomed this bonus throng of shooters following the traditional close of the tourist season in September. The Better Business Bureaus of Camdenton and Osage Beach were both involved in promoting the tournament.

I often towed my bass boat for both the State Shoot and Fall Handicap, a 20' Skeeter equipped with 135 hp Evinrude Silver Starflite motor. Early morning or late afternoon fishing for bass could be productive, plus it was just very pleasant being out on the lake.

Many evenings were spent around the Breezewood Resort telling fishing stories. One of the best storytellers was C.E. Barnhart, Kansas City's many time trapshooting All-American. Any time there was someone new amongst us, Barney liked to tell the story of the one-armed fisherman. The one-armed fisherman was out on the lake one day, fishing along the bank in a cove while under a canopy of oak trees that extended out overhead. A squirrel made a jump from one tree to the next and end up a little short. The squirrel fell into the boat and bounced into the open tackle box. With lures clinging to his body he jumped into the lake swimming frantically and was soon devoured by the most enormous Largemouth Bass the one-armed fisherman had ever seen. Later, when asked just how large the fish appeared to be, the fisherman held up his one arm in front of him and said- "he was this long".

For many years the Fall Handicap was held in early October, often coinciding with Major League Baseball's World Series. The background consisted mostly of hardwood trees that started the week leafed in green, then transitioned to yellow and orange during the course of the week. Typical Missouri weather during that time of year could be delightful or just plain nasty and change in a moment's notice.

Club Manager Burlie Wilson and wife Olabell hosted this event for the MTA, along with their Board of Directors. Burlie and Olabell attended many popular trapshooting tournaments around the country promoting the Fall Handicap, personally inviting shooters to come and visit them in October. For many years, attendees were treated to a hog roast on Saturday night along with the Special Event. The shooting and vendor base grew tremendously during this period.

In early October of 2000, Bob Schultz, NC, Ralph Pfeifer, IL, and I provided the Canterbury Voice Release systems at the Missouri Fall

Handicap for the first time. I towed my travel trailer out from Nevada and stayed on the grounds for about 10 days.

When I arrived, it was extremely warm for that time of year and the A/C in the RV was a blessing as temps reached 90 degrees. Ten days later it was so cold my propane ran out during the night while running the heater. Temperatures had plummeted to mid-20s. Along with this, shooters experienced strong northerly winds and cold temperatures for the weekend events. Over 2100 shooters were classified that week. A total of 1651 competed in Saturday's handicap event; the winner posted a lone score of 96. There were 1390 in Sunday's handicap and a lone score of 95 at the top.

I don't believe anyone ever attended the Missouri Fall Handicap tournament with the hope of shooting for higher averages. Odds were that it was going to be a very challenging week. The vast majority of shooters attending this event were there for the money. A score of 94 or 95 in either of the final two handicaps would pay very well. A 25-straight might exceed $1000, and a 50-straight might exceed $3000. Burlie did an excellent job of setting the targets for such an event.

However, all good things must come to an end, and I sadly witnessed part of this during one of my final visits in 2003 or 2004.

During a conversation with one of the long-time MTA Board Members, he stated they needed to bring someone else in to run the facility. Hopefully new management would be capable of setting decent targets. I had known this gentleman for forty years and could hardly believe what I was hearing but assumed there was more at play than was being conveyed. Why would any responsible person change a tournament structure and management that had achieved such overwhelming success? The Board Member was a long-time Senior shooter and certainly had his pulse on what was happening in Missouri, but I felt this may have a catastrophic impact on the Fall Handicap as a money- oriented tournament. It's also possible he had listened to recommendations from several disgruntled All-Americans unable to perform well at this event and threatening an ultimatum- "Either throw decent targets or were not returning."

The overwhelming majority of the shooters attending the Missouri Fall Handicap during its peak years were not All-American shooters.

Sure enough, Burlie was indeed let go, and replaced with a new manager.

A considerable number of things happened during the years that followed, but all to a gradual demise of the Missouri Fall Handicap being recognized as a premier money shoot. None of this was due to the hard work and efforts performed by their new manager. However, Pat Traps, voice release systems, and moving a few weeks earlier all led to higher scores, and reduced payouts. Times had changed. A tournament that once hosted over 2000 shooters at its peak drew less than 400 for their 2019 event. Sadly, the bulk of the shooters, and the money that drew them, had departed. At least for the time being.

Everything tends to run in cycles and that's certainly the case for many gun clubs. The MTA grounds are among the finest in the country and the surrounding Ozark community provides a tremendous array of accommodations and recreational opportunities. I have no doubt this facility will become extremely popular again but perhaps not as the money shoot of earlier years.

The ATA Midwestern Satellite Grand originated at this location many years ago prior to becoming the Fall Handicap of today. I wouldn't be surprised at all if this should come full circle and a

Satellite Grand return to this facility. At this point and time, it might be an excellent fit.

ELLIOTT'S SHOOTING PARK

Derived from a live pigeon club on the Blue River, then located in Raytown, MO, Elliott's was my home grounds, along with many well-known shooters before me. The clubhouse had large windows across the entirety of the north side and a large stone fireplace located in the center of the south wall. Photos of champions from decades before decorated the wood-paneled walls and areas above the windows. There was a very small locker room on the west end of the building where some of the older shooters kept their aimin' oil. There were 4 trap fields, plus one practice trap/skeet combo field to the west, separated from the event fields by a maintenance building. The Elliott family home was on the east end of the grounds.

Elliott's was the very first gun club I ever visited and certainly set high standards for future expectations. It was perfect in every way and had an atmosphere like no other. It became a major part of my life and I lived within a mile of it for over eight years.

It seemed Russ Elliott and Jack Thompson were there during all open hours, welcoming shooters and signing them up for practice or a variety of club programs that were offered. Every starting round was announced over the PA directing the shooters to the correct field. The same announcements were made for every practice round. Elliott's was the home of the K.C.T.A., or Kansas City Trapshooter's Association.

Elliott's had a long history of producing champions. The youngest ever to win the Clay Target Championship at Vandalia, Kevin Onka, was from nearby Sugar Creek. Kevin was only 16 years old when he defeated C.E. Barnhart of Kansas City in shoot-off for the title in 1959. Four years later, Barney claimed the title for himself, defeating George Snellenberger and Dan Orlich in shoot-off in 1963.

I shot many targets at Elliott's and always considered it one of the tougher places to post a score. Background was good, but the targets were always leaning towards maximum distance and angle spread. Anywhere else seemed easier, Vandalia no exception, and may explain the number of champions that came from this club.

There were several registered tournaments during the year; major events being the Interstate Shoot and the Mo-Kan. The Interstate was a classic featuring the "Diamond Button Handicap" and the Mo-Kan final handicap featured a new automobile to the winner. I attended my second Missouri State Shoot held on the four trap fields at Elliott's in 1963.

Wednesday nights offered the same programs for many years. "Meat Races" started at 6pm, with six shooters per race (one starting "in the hole" behind station 1) Two shots were required per post for a total of 10. Ties shot-off from the porch 35 yards behind the trap house. There was a total of ten "Meat Races" every Wednesday evening. Once they were completed, the next event was a "Protection Race". This was a pick-your partner buddy-buddy shoot. Following the "Protection Race" was the 25-target derby, shot from your assigned ATA yardage or known ability.

Jay Smith became a long-time manager of the facility. One of his staffers was Lynn Gipson, now Executive Director of the ATA. Lynn started as a trap boy and worked his way inside to be the main cashier, then eventually Assistant Manager, and finally, Manager, following Jay's retirement.

In the early 80s, local trap shooter Vern Hill, purchased Elliott's and within a year added on to the clubhouse and expanded the trap fields to a total of 14. Vern also established Racer targets, a new clay target with a manufacturing plant within a mile of the shooting park. Racer targets were also used at the 1983 Grand American.

Unfortunately, an unrelated business venture required Elliott's to be used as collateral. The unrelated business failed and Elliott's and Racer both fell victims. The old club closed, was eventually torn down and all trap fields removed. The property later become the home of a convalescent center.

Under efforts spearheaded by local shooter Joby Jobson and several other local shooters, the Kansas City Trapshooters Association eventually relocated to the newly built Smithville Gun Club north of Kansas City and part of the Smithville Lake development. Lynn Gipson continued there as manager until he took the Executive Director position with the A.T.A.

DENVER METRO TRAP & SKEET / MILE-HI SHOOTING PARK

Located a few miles north of downtown Denver, DMT&S became the second home of the Mile-High Trapshooting Tournament, following the in-town location at Sloan's Lake. The first manager I can remember at DMT&S was Roscoe Abrams.

From 1976 through 1981, I tried to make it to Denver three times each year. This was an easy 8-hour drive from Kansas City with hardly a bend in the interstate. The Centennial Shoot was Memorial Day weekend, the Colorado State Shoot was mid-June, and the Mile-Hi was the last of July.

For many years there was a tiny bar area that served as the center of social activity following the day's events. If I remember correctly, there may have been only six or eight barstools, but a huge number of shooters congregated in this crowded area to enjoy one another's company. This was on the second floor of the clubhouse that offered panoramic views of the shooting fields and the Rocky Mountains to the west. I made many new friends at this facility; Pete Labella, Sammy Spano and Lee Kastle, just to name a few. I believe this may be where I first met Tony DeSimone as he was a resident of nearby Louisville. Tony was trained in Italy at the Perazzi factory and was instrumental in Perazzi's early success in the U.S. If you attended a major trapshooting tournament in the West or Southwest in the 1970s & 1980s, you could count on Tony being there providing impeccable service.

Few were aware that Tony was a master chef, and for years invited huge crowds over to his house for fabulous Italian dinners. Over the years these events hosted an increasing number of trap shooters and their families. Eventually Tony leased one of the banks in Louisville to have enough room to successfully throw his party.

Tony's an amazing and accomplished individual that's participated in the Boston Marathon several times and holds a third-degree Black Belt in karate. For those of you familiar with the "Big Texan" steakhouse in Amarillo, TX, Tony has completed the monster 72 oz steak challenge on two different occasions.

Tony and I have remained lifelong friends to this day.

Another of my very best friends, Wayne Leslie, lived on the southeast side of Denver in Aurora. Wayne always extended an open invitation to share his home when I attended Denver events. Wayne became a lifelong fishing friend and we made many trips to Lake Powell and Alaska together. He would also serve as best man at my wedding in 1983. Wayne passed away in May 2017, at the age of 86.

There were too many memorable moments at the Mile-Hi facility to recall them all, but I do remember one very well.

It was a 300-target day, with doubles first, handicap second and the 16-yard event third. Gene Sears was on the squad, along with big Charlie Sheckler (PA). Gene ran the 100 doubles in the morning. He also ran the first 75 straight in the handicap. After continuing straight on the first four stations of the final trap, we're about to move to our last post when Charlie goes running over to him with his right hand extended and shouting- "Great job Gene!" Gene said something like "thanks, but we've got 5 more to go." Totally embarrassed, Charlie cringed noticeably and slunk back over to his post. Fortunately, Gene continued to run the 100 in handicap which I believe was his first. Unfortunately, he missed the first target out in the 16-yard event to end up with a 299 x 300 for the day.

It was during this same period that Gene Sears, Randy Pennington, and Ray Stafford purchased the facility. Ray served as manager and established his gun sales there which continued for many years.

Always good tournaments with good payouts, and usually good scores if you could avoid a late afternoon squall which was common during the Mile Hi tournament.

Unfortunately, insurance issues coupled with a group of local rowdies, eventually led to the closing of the bar. While understandable, the tournaments never seemed quite the same after the bar disappeared. A place where so many had created good times and fond memories was now gone forever.

PHOENIX TRAP & SKEET CLUB

The original Phoenix Trap & Skeet Club was organized in the 1930s and located in Echo Canyon at the base of Camelback Mountain. The facility most of us were familiar with in the 1970s was derived from a Winchester Gun Club located on the West side of Phoenix just off Indian School Road. I first attended the Midwinter Chain tournament there in 1976 and enjoyed the facility immensely. I'm sure part of this was due to escaping the harsh January weather in the Kansas City area. I always enjoyed the post New Year's drive from the Midwest to the Southwest. Once you had left New Mexico travelling west through the 4-corners area, blue skies and warmer temperatures prevailed, even allowing the car windows to be rolled down for the first time in months.

There were several times that I arrived at the Phoenix club on a Sunday afternoon just in time to catch the Super Bowl being broadcast at the large L-shaped bar. I can't remember exactly which year, but it was the Dallas Cowboys vs the Denver Broncos. The place was absolutely packed with fans representing both teams and everyone was having a good time. There was a multitude of clubs with bars in this era which seemed to provide such outstanding social interaction. So politically incorrect these days, as are so many things we enjoyed in the past.

Shooting conditions were usually outstanding at Phoenix T & S. This was assuming you didn't squad too early as the club faced straight east.

On one occasion, I was shooting a 16-yard event at this facility with Ray Stafford and Wayne Leslie, probably 1976. I can't remember for sure if it was the Winter Chain or Arizona State shoot. We were down towards the north end of the line. Once we took the field, I noticed some type of rodent moving around in front of the trap house. It appeared he was in the chipmunk/ground squirrel family. He would appear momentarily, then dart back out of sight. I tried to ignore it, but he was persistent and tended to pop out at about the time you were calling for your target. This went on for the first post or two, and finally, Ray missed a target. If you look back at ATA shoot records for 1976-1977, this was a very rare occurrence. Ray hardly ever missed a 16-yard target during this period. Shortly after the miss, Ray was about to shoot again when the rodent made a run for it with apparent intentions of making it to the trap house to our right. He didn't make it. Ray torched a round off and the furry distraction disappeared in a cloud of desert dust. The little girl keeping score let out a blood curdling shriek, broke into tears, jumped down off the scoring chair and ran off the field. We found out the departed was her little friend. She and her loader in the trap house had been feeding him for days. The scorekeeper refused to return and score for us. The line referee eventually found a replacement and we completed the round.

A couple of unfortunate incidents also occurred at this facility. The first was during the last event of the Spring Grand in 1977 or 1978. A shooter was closing his Perazzi TM1 for his next shot when the stock came off in his hand. This resulted in the closed action, barrel and forearm doing a 180-degree pivot as it hit the ground and fired back into the area of on-deck shooters. Unfortunately, the discharge struck Kitty Weitkamp, a lady shooter from Wyoming among others. Kitty sustained damage to one arm. The worst injury occurred to a young man that just happened to be riding by on one of the trolley wagons being pulled by tractors. He took a single pellet and lost the sight of an eye.

The second incident involved a LaPorte trap display in the vendor area during a Spring Grand many years later. A gentleman and his family just happened to walk by when one of the traps discharged striking him in the hand. Initially it appeared to be of minor consequence until it was revealed the injured party was a neurosurgeon from South Africa. This ended up in multiple lawsuits, obviously with no winners.

Like so many other facilities of its type, the Phoenix Trap & Skeet Club eventually succumbed to urban sprawl in the early 2000s. Another renowned facility of the golden years of trapshooting and birthplace of the ATA Spring Grand. Once lost, and never to be replaced.

VANDALIA

Vandalia, OH, was the epicenter of the trapshooting world at the time I was first exposed to the sport in 1959. As I accompanied my father, Stan, to Elliott's Shooting Park in Raytown, MO, I overheard stories from those that had been to Vandalia on previous occasions. This was trapshooting's Utopia and you simply couldn't call yourself a trap shooter until you had been christened at the hallowed grounds. The sheer size alone was impressive with a total of 48 fields spread out along the south side of the Dayton Airport.

I made my first trip in 1961, along with my folks. Dad had been registering targets for over a year and was shooting well.

Travelling in a 1955 Cadillac Coupe De Ville on highway U.S. 40 the entire way, we stayed at the Crossroads Motel a mile east of grounds. Dad promised if he broke 98 or better in one of the three big handicaps, I would have a new Model 12 Winchester when we returned home. He did, earning a 4th place finish in the Grand American Handicap. He also kept his promise.

We returned in 1963. At this point I had been registering targets for about 18 months as a Sub-Junior. A few weeks before the Grand I entered my first 100 straight at the Southwestern Zone Championships, plus won the final handicap with a 96. I had been punched to 19.5 yards.

I met Frank Little for the first time a month later as he was at the handicap table in Vandalia. I presented him with my card. He reviewed it, then punched me to the 21-yard line and wished me good luck!

The grounds were amazing. On the far west end, small aircraft landed on the grass and parked next to the practice traps. The Ljutic building was also in this vicinity in 1963.

California's Gene Lumsden and I shot off for a Junior award following Tuesday's Class singles race, and Reno's Jimmy Hunter and I shot-off for Junior Champion of Champions. It was a great week. Gene, Jimmy and I have remained friends for many years.

I would attend 35 more Grands at Vandalia before it made the move to Sparta, IL in 2006. So many memorable moments that it would be hard to list all of them, but I'll take a shot at it; chronologically if possible-

- Banners: When coming into Vandalia, there were always large welcome banners overhead from one side of the street to the other. These would include the ATA logo and the Vandalia Chamber of Commerce. There was no other place in the world that trap shooters felt more welcome and appreciated.

- Home Ground Entryway: When you entered the grounds, one of the first things you noticed was the manager's home located immediately to the right of the driveway. I believe David Bopp may have been the last occupant and the structure was eventually torn down.

- Chalk Leaderboards: On the north side of the original Central Handicap Building, and east of the grandstands, were the large chalk leaderboards. These were elevated 10-12 feet off the ground and two or three college-aged kids manned this area daily. As scores came in during the day, the top scores would be posted at this location. You could always find a mob of people below pointing up and taking photographs of the leaders as their names were being posted. These names and scores changed constantly during the day requiring a considerable amount of erasing and re-writing.

- Main Scoreboard Area: This was a large, open-air metal building about a half-mile west of the Central Handicap Building at that time. The large scoreboards ran right down the center in an east-west configuration and were 2-sided. There was an elevated deck for personnel. All the scoresheets would be posted prior to the next event, indicating squad numbers and squad members, yardages, class, etc., but absent of scores. All scores were entered later; manually. As scoresheets came in and were approved in the nearby "Trap and Field" office, they eventually made their way out to be posted. One person would read them off, the other would enter them on the board. It would sound something like this- "Next squad #142; ready, 23, dot, 24, dot, 24." This continued until all four sub-event scores had been recorded for each shooter. The "dots" represented 25-straights and would be stamped in red following each posting. Anyone posting 100 or 200-straight would have all their sub event and total scores represented by the red stamps. The "Trap & Field" office was also located in this building.

- Tractors & Wagon: Tractors & wagons served as people-movers. There were no 4-trap banks at this time. Everyone that shot on the odd numbered traps went one direction for the entire length, or you shot on the even traps and went the other way. Your fields were usually five or six fields apart so shooters and spectators had to do a considerable amount of walking.

- Doubles: A hundred target doubles event required shooting on four different fields; 30-20-30-20. This was standard procedure at most clubs at the time.

- The Beer Tent: This is where you went to find someone, especially once the shooting was completed for the day. Everyone visited the beer tent, featuring Cincinnati-brewed Hudepohl beer on tap for many years before transitioning to Budweiser. There often seemed to be a competition between tables on who could stack the empty beer cups the highest. Great sandwiches and other snacks were also available at this area. At the end of the day the tractors and wagons all parked right in front of the beer tent next to the green rail fence.

- The Cafeteria: I can remember the same ladies staffing the cafeteria for many years. The cafeteria was always clean and provided excellent food at a fair price. The only drawback, whatever temperatures and humidity were felt outside would also be inside. Screen doors and screened windows provided subtle relief, along with fans. Eventually air conditioning was added.

- The Campers: No, not RVs, most of the campers in the 1960s were staying in large tents. I can remember the huge Pennsylvania and Ohio tents having many shooters bringing their cots and staying overnight in these tents. The main bathroom facility next to the Central Entry Building was equipped with showers.

- Shoot-offs: Shoot-offs would be called late every afternoon. Multiple grandstands would fill with spectators. This is where you finally were able to see the top shooters you had read and heard about. Representatives from all the ammunition companies were visible at tables in front of the spectators.

- Herb Orre: Herb occupied a tiny wooden building just east of the cafeteria, installing his famous Orre chokes and Super-chokes with a reamer. The vast majority of his work would have been done on the Winchester Model 12s that were so prevalent during the 60s.

- Troy: Troy, OH, and the Troy Gun Club were just a few miles north of Vandalia. During the main days of the Grand American, the Troy club hosted a 100-bird handicap program during the day and a 50-bird night program that was infamous. Practice traps were also available during the day. For the 50-bird night program, everyone shot at 25 targets from 16 yards, then a second 25 from a yardage represented by the score on your first round. Depending on scores and yardage differences, you may be on a different squad for the second round. The targets were fast and wide, and the lighting less than perfect. Every night, part of the entry went into a 50-straight progressive jackpot that continued to grow if no score of 50 was obtained. 50-straights were extremely rare. Half of the accumulative jackpot money would be provided to Thursday night, and half to Friday night, paid out to the high scores each of these final two nights. The crowds were massive on Thursday & Friday nights and shooting often continued until 2am until local ordinances were eventually passed. There was a small restaurant within walking distance packed with shooters having a snack and waiting for their time to shoot. I believe there was an entire group of shooters that attended the Grand every year due to the Troy club and the programs they offered.

- Christies: Right across the street in the small strip mall south of the ATA grounds was Christies. Known primarily as a pizza place, it offered a variety of good food and filled up every afternoon and evening during the Grand. A great atmosphere and probably the second-best place to find an acquaintance if unsuccessful at the beer tent. The owners surely dreaded seeing the Grand American come to an end each year.

- Name Badges: All attendees were eligible to receive a custom name badge. Typewriters were used on labels that were slipped into a holder with a ribbon and ATA pin designating the year. In the late 60s the pin also included the name of the current ATA President.

- Vendors: Any business associated with the shotgun sports had vendor areas during the Grand American. A few of the larger vendors had permanent buildings, but many were tent vendors. Most of these were to the west of the beer tent, but a few on the east side of the central entry building once past the vendor building. The main buildings to the west were for Bob Allen, Krieghoff and Mec. To the East, Ithaca, Winchester, Remington, Federal and Anton.

The Grand Americans of this era were certainly "Grand"

THOSE ALONG THE EARLY TRAIL

ERNEST JELLEY

I've elected to start off this section with a name unheard of by the majority of modern-day trap shooters. An accomplished shooter himself, Ernest Jelley captured all three Missouri State Championships- Singles, Handicap and Doubles, between 1943 and 1953, and became President of the Amateur Trapshooting Association in 1960. He was inducted into the Missouri Trapshooting Hall of Fame in 1978.

What I remember best about him was his friendliness and willingness to approach and encourage new shooters into the sport of trapshooting. He would go out of his way to offer advice and make everyone feel welcome. He was ATA Delegate for the State of Missouri for 20 years, even following his ATA Presidency, and truly knew the shooters in his region.

In the early 1960s, you could shoot six days or nights a week in the Kansas City area. Local gun clubs included- Elliott's Shooting Park, the Owl Gun Club, Riverside Gun Club, Schroeder's, and 7 & 10. You could drive an extra 30-45 minutes and shoot at Cedar Hill, Ottawa, or the Winchester Gun Club in Bucyrus, KS.

Ernest made it his job to visit not only the clubs mentioned above, but all the clubs in his State.

Ernest Jelley was also a businessman and manufactured clay targets in Kansas City, Missouri. The "Bobwhite" was the predominant target of this area.

My father and I visited the "plant" on 21st & Harrison Street in 1961. It was an old multi-level building, poorly air-conditioned. What I remember most was the painting of the targets. As the targets came off the press and down a conveyor belt, there were employees waiting with a paint can and paint brushes in hand. Two of the workers applied the yellow paint to the dome of the passing clays with a single, circular swish. The other employee painted the complete top of about every third or fourth target solid white. All used what appeared to be 4" paint brushes, continually dipping into the cans. This type of work must have made for a very long day.

By the time the yellow-domed targets reached the end of the line, they were immediately stacked, each stack wrapped with a page from the daily newspaper, and finally placed into boxes. The white targets had to dry a little longer on a rack before being wrapped allowing ample time for them to properly dry. Otherwise they would be stuck together when pulled out for use.

The Bobwhite target manufacturing company eventually sold to Richard Cannady and the operation was moved to Ottawa, KS.

Like any amateur sport that offers something of value to win, trapshooting also had its "sandbaggers". These were short-yardage shooters that made a career of staying at short-yardage. Their game was always to break a lucrative front or back 49 or 50 straight in a handicap event without having a score high enough to earn yardage. (There were no middle 50's back in those days). When you consider that most shooters played all the options and purses, substantial money was at stake. Obviously, this meant sloughing off targets at some point during a 100-target handicap event. They tended to squad late in events and were aware of what kind of scores were posted before they took the firing line.

As a man of integrity, Ernest considered this cheating and was determined to do something about it.

During this period, ATA State Delegates had the authority to adjust a shooter's handicap yardage on the spot if justified. I witnessed Ernest do this very thing after watching a suspected sandbagger for months.

It was during a large handicap event in eastern Kansas in 1966. The suspect was a Missouri shooter and had missed one target on the first field, then 25, 25, before starting his final round. There were several scores of 98 and 97 already posted, but a 99 would have the top of the purse all to itself, and to a sandbagger; justified taking a yard punch.

The shooter walked to his final post, now 20 straight on the final field. He lost his 96th target. He then missed his 97th, 98th, 99th, and 100th target to end with a final score of 94, and just under the total score earning a punch. He had no idea he was being closely observed.

Delegate Jelley was ready. When the shooter came off the line, Ernie offered his condolences, stating how he just knew the shooter was going to do it this time. He also asked if he could see his handicap card which he immediately punched two additional yards. "Congratulations on a good attempt and better luck next time!"

Anyone visiting Ernest's home would certainly be introduced to "Splash", his beloved black Labrador Retriever. Ernie was always eager to demonstrate what Splash was capable of. "Splash, go in the other room and bring back a red towel." Splash would wander off, wagging his tail, and sure enough returned with a red towel. "Now, go and find me a yellow towel." Once again, off he would go off and come back with a yellow towel. This would be repeated with two or three additional colors surely convincing anyone that might be in doubt. Dogs were most definitely not color-blind, at least not this one.

On the wall of the old Elliott's clubhouse, there hung a plaque with a picture of Ernest and Splash on it. Below the picture was the story of how Ernest fell through the ice during a duck hunting trip and would have surely perished if Splash hadn't been there to save him. It was a story that led to my relationships with multiple Black Labrador Retrievers that has spanned several decades.

Ernest Jelley was just one of the gentlemen trap shooters that made such a memorable impression on me as a youngster entering the game. Like so many other unsung role models in my home area, always willing to lend a hand and offer encouraging words. Splendid men representing values that youth should certainly aspire to.

I'm forever in their debt.

DAN ORLICH

I had the opportunity to shoot with the great Dan Orlich on several occasions during the GWG, and at least twice at Bob Taylors in Las Vegas. One of these times was at the GWG in the late 70s and Dan was leading off our squad. He mentioned he had been struggling a bit with singles prior to the tournament, but I certainly never foresaw what was coming. We were shooting the first 16-yard event of the week and sure enough Dan missed two on the first trap. He was bewildered by this as we all were and talked about it while moving to our second field which was directly in front of the clubhouse.

Dan Orlich was trapshooting's Arnold Palmer, and his presence on the trap field always drew a large crowd of spectators. This day was no exception.

The first post of the second 25 was uneventful, but as we're shooting along, I noticed a meadowlark flying back and forth out in front of us. There were stakes in the ground in front of each trap field to designate the 50-yard markers used for setting the proper target distance. The meadowlark was flying back and forth from stake to stake. As Dan called for his second target on post 2, the meadowlark flew from the distance stake on the trap to our right, to the distance stake on our trap. Dan drew a straightaway, missed, and the meadowlark plummeted to the ground. Orlich yelled "Jesus Christ, did you see that? I knew I was shooting to the left!" Of course, I realized exactly what Orlich was talking about as I had seen the meadowlark fall almost 70 yards in front of us. After a few snickers, everyone finally collected themselves and we continued the round. However, for the entire remainder of the round, about every 30 seconds or so, one of the meadowlarks wings would raise up as if waving at us.

On another occasion, possibly the same year, we were shooting handicap and arrived at our last trap, way down on the east side of the canal. It had been cloudy all day and the visibility proved to be extremely challenging. It became even worse about halfway through our last round.

This was back when the Golden West Grand used to throw a black target with a small white center, often referred to as the "poker chip" target.

We settled in on our third post and as leadoff, Orlich called for his target to start the sequence. The target went out, but barely visible. Orlich put his gun down and started over again with the same result, and finally a third time. He paused, looked over at the scorekeeper and very pleasantly asked if she could hear him. At this time, Bonillas spoke up "Uh, Orlich, there's been three perfectly good targets go out already." Orlich was amazed "Holy Christ, ok, let's try this again. When I call pull, you guys yell right or left!"

Dan was leading our squad when I broke what I felt was the best handicap score of my ATA tournament shooting career.

It was at Bob Taylor's "100 Grand" in 1979, during Saturday's "100 Grand" handicap. The wind was blowing strong out of the northwest and it was cold. It was difficult enough just finding warm shooting attire for such a day that allowed you the ability to handle the gun properly. Obviously, long underwear was necessary, plus I wore a black wool turtleneck sweater and insulated ski pants.

The targets during that event were climbing high to the left, straightaways were sliding to the right, and right angles were diving. You couldn't rely just on instincts, but rather had to assess each target individually, and quickly. Left to right pattern drift appeared to be 3 to 4 feet. This resulted in a mentally and physically exhausting event.

I managed to scratch out a 95 with 49 out of the last 50. I was completely worn out. I had parked my car down behind our last trap. When we finished, Dan rode back towards the clubhouse with me. He asked how I had finished and when I told him he immediately said that was without a doubt, a winning score. He was correct, and it held up by itself with over 800 entries. Along with a Superbowl-style ring to Champion, the score provided a very lucrative payoff, and not just for the purse, as 25's and 49s were also extremely rare that day. Considering current dollar values, the total payoff for this one score in that windblown event would be comparable to just over $38,000 today. This was why yesterday's shooters were willing to take the line in less than perfect conditions.

As stated earlier, there was something of value to shoot for during this period, and the expenses were considerably less. At the 1979 Grand American, targets were $30 per 100, and that **included** four boxes of premium ammunition.

Many years later, Dan was one of the first persons I encountered when coming in through the back door of the Phoenix Trap & Skeet Club. I had just arrived for the Spring Grand. Dan flagged me down, walked over and said "Steve, you're not going to believe what happened yesterday!" This was about as excited as I had ever seen Dan Orlich about anything. The first thing that went through my mind was that he had broken 100 in a handicap event earlier in the week.

He goes on to tell me that he had his first hole-in-one at golf the day before!

I've nothing but the fondest memories of Dan Orlich, and his role as the premier ambassador of trapshooting. Plus, how many people can say they've actually been on a squad with an ex-Green Bay Packer that played under Curly Lambeau?

PHIL ROSS

Inside the clubhouse at the old Golden West Grand following a day's shooting in 1980, the bar and entire clubhouse area was packed as was typical of this era. Several of my squad mates and myself were at the east end of the old rustic bar enjoying the camaraderie when California shooter Russ Lewis walked up to visit with us.

Russ was a bit bleary-eyed and appeared to have already been at the bar for some time. In his hand, Russ was holding a rolled-up copy of the current "Trap & Field" magazine. "I don't believe it" he said, referring to the magazine. "Have you read what he said?" The "he" that was being referred to was Phil Ross and the "what he said" referred to a comment Phil had made during a "Trap & Field" interview following his Vandalia Handicap and High-Over-All win at the 1979 Grand American. Among other things, Phil had stated he could run the 100-yard dash in 10 seconds. Russ went on "I don't frickin' believe it, I can't run 100 yards in 10 seconds, and I know I can outrun him!" Russ was light-to-medium build and appeared he could probably move around a track reasonably well. Phil, well, during these years Phil was pretty good sized, maybe 350 pounds or better. By now, others around us were tuning in as the volume of Russ's words was elevating. At this point Russ wandered over into the area of card tables and sure enough, Phil was there playing Hearts with Bobby Gilbertson, Don Ewing, and some others. Russ openly challenged Phil at this point and Phil peaked up from his cards and very gentlemanly responded "Now Russ, be careful what you're getting yourself into here."

Russ's response was that he'd bet 100 bucks he could outrun Phil in a foot race. That did it. Phil accepted the challenge and 2/3 of the clubhouse occupants immediately emptied out of the north door onto the field directly in front of the clubhouse.

The course was laid out for 100 yards running from East to West right across the middle of a couple of trap fields. A starter was selected; "Ready, set, go" and they were off. Phil pulled an unbelievable jump off the starting line and immediately left Russ ten feet behind. Awe-struck, Russ conceded immediately and paid off, stating "I would have never believed he could move like that". Phil didn't escape unscathed though. His initial jump off the line resulted in blowing the thighs right out of both legs of this pants. His trousers were a total loss.

During a GWG handicap event about this same period, our squad had completed the first 50 targets and was now crossing the canal by the shell room. As we're walking along, I noticed Bobby Gilbertson coming towards us from the opposite direction, gun and shell bag over his shoulder. He had a big smile on his face. He pulled me aside, almost hysterical, and said "You're not going to believe what just happened on our last trap."

Bobby and Phil travelled and shot together for several years, pooling their resources, sharing costs, and splitting their winnings between them. He went on to explain they had just started their last trap of the handicap event and Phil was having trouble with the puller. (keep in mind, this was years before voice release systems. Someone was required to physically push a button on the end of a cord, promptly at the shooter's command, then accurately score the results. You'll have to do some research in trapshooting archives to find out why this person wasn't referred to as a "pusher!"). Bobby described the puller as a young man age 18-20, that acted as if he would much rather be anywhere else. Phil explained to the puller that he called for his target using an array of calls which may sound like "Pull, yup, hype, etc." The puller nodded to acknowledge what Phil was telling him and they proceeded. After two or three more attempts to receive a target, Phil finally looked back over at him and asked the puller if he had a problem. The response was "f_ _ _ you, you fat s.o.b." Phil raised his eyebrows, handed his Model 12 to Bobby, and headed towards the puller. The young man leaped out of the scoring chair, ran south across the tractor path, and sailed over the barb wire fence separating the club grounds from a pasture. To everyone's amazement, Phil sailed over the fence likewise, with the puller running as hard as he could and Phil in hot pursuit. They eventually both disappeared from sight over a hill, hundreds of yards away and heading towards Reno.

About ten minutes went by and a lone figure was spotted heading back towards the club. It was Phil. Everything was backed up at this point on several fields as all shooting had ceased. It took him a while, but Phil finally reached the fence, climbed over for the second time, and approached the field. He was breathing hard and needed just a few moments to collect himself. After a few minutes, he regained his composure, picked his Model 12 out of the rack, looked around and said- "I guess we need another puller."

I'm unaware if the status of the first puller was ever revealed or determined. This incident subsequently earned Phil the nickname "Huff 'n Puff" which stayed with him for many years thereafter.

Phil was certainly one of the better golfers amongst our group of duffers. This wasn't saying much. In Denver the week of the Mile High, Phil, Bobby Gilbertson, Britt Robinson and myself hit the links during one of the prelim days. Phil made a lot of very good shots and sunk one of the craziest putts I've ever seen made by anyone. It was about a 50-footer with four or five left-right breaks and an elevation drop before reaching the cup. Phil applied a considerable amount of body English to encourage the ball along on its track. Absolutely amazing, and the highlight of our day.

Phil would also attempt to mess with his competitor's head if the opportunity arose. At the completion of the 1979, Mile-High tournament in Denver, Phil and Denver's top handicap shooter had tied for the final handicap event following scores of 99. There was a tremendous amount of interest in this shoot-off as it was "that big guy from California" versus the homeboy. Once the shoot-off was called, a throng of onlookers gathered behind the field and the upper deck of the clubhouse.

Phil and his opponent entered the field and checked the scoresheets to verify their starting positions. Phil was leading off. They settled in on the traditional post 2 and 4 and looked at a couple of targets. The previously noisy group of spectators became as quiet as church mice.

Then, Phil glanced over and said- "You know if you miss one it's all over." I believe his opponent was taken aback by this but refused to acknowledge. The first two targets for each of them were uneventful, then his opponent lost the third target out. Phil closed his Model 12, started to mount the gun, but then opened the action and took it back down. He looked over, almost apologetically and said- "So soon?" Phil went on to break the 25 and the two departed the field without the customary handshake. Psyche, with the ability to back it up, is a powerful tool.

TOM SEITZ

I never met a finer person than C.C. "Tom" Seitz. I don't remember exactly when we first met but became friends immediately. I spent many, many hours on the phone with Tom in the mid-70's as he helped me develop a doubles gun that I could consistently perform with. After winning the Grand American Doubles Championship in 1974 with a 30" Browning Lightning, (with considerable modifications done by Charlie Mount at Simmons Guns) I moved on to a 30" Perazzi MX8, then switched to a 32", then back to the 30" but wasn't finding a solution I was confident in. Plus, I realized I needed something that impacted higher than what was currently available on the market. After thousands of rounds, and numerous phone calls, I finally felt I had a definite direction. I sent Tom a 32" inch MX8. He was able to cut the barrels back to about 31 ¼", then back-bore and re-choke. I also had him overlay a new rib that was ¼" higher at the back then taper down to the existing rib height at the muzzle. An adjustable comb on the stock brought everything together. The genius and machining skills of Tom Seitz made this possible. My best success in doubles was achieved when using this separate gun instead of a combo. My ideal stock length and height for doubles was 1/8" longer, and 1/8" lower than the stock on the TM1 I used for 16 yard and handicap, while the barrel for both guns patterned a full 100% high.

During one of the early Southern Grands at Florida's Silver Dollar club, Tom and I were conversing in the pro shop. This was back when everything was on the west side of the road. Club owner Bill Jacobsen came out and we visited with him for a while, then he invited us back into the secret gun vault. This was an amazing place. Lighted display cases of dozens and dozens of the finest pump guns ever made; Winchester Model 12s & Model 42s, and Remington Model 31s. Every one of these were highly engraved and the majority with gold inlay. A simply stunning collection. Then, on the wall bordering the east side of the room was nothing but original Seitz single-barrel trap guns; fifteen in all if I remember correctly. This was a staggering number when you consider Tom Seitz only built 45 of these during his lifetime. Bill left us for a moment, and I remember asking Tom "What goes through your mind when you see all of these up there?" He thought about it for a moment then said- "I guess I would really prefer to see them out on the field being used." It made perfect sense to me considering he produced these fine shotguns at a rate of only about six per year.

Tom dropped by the Missouri Fall Handicap in October of 1978. He had flown to Florida and purchased an older Revcon motor home from a retired couple that had kept it in pristine condition. He left it parked at the club one afternoon and Leo Harrison III and Martin Wilbur discovered he had left the keys in it. They took it for a test run and discovered multiple packages of pop bottle rockets inside. The result was an RV heading down highway "A" impersonating a mobile firework show. Of course, Tom found out and a series of pranks, which included deflating the perp's tires among other things, followed during the course of the following week. This culminated with a phone call I received from Tom after he had arrived back home in Oregon about a week later. He said as he was driving along, at some point he turned on the heater fan and a horrible odor permeated the rig. He suspected that Leo and Martin might have had something to do with it. Sure enough, I found out later they had planted a few small fish in several hidden locations of the RV. They had the last laugh, and Tom had a very fishy smelling RV for several weeks.

In 1979, I proposed another challenge to Tom. I wanted to have a 35" barrel built to fit my TM1. Many long yardage shooters at the time, including myself, were shooting guns with barrels bent upwards to raise the point of impact, and having a great deal of success. Bending the barrel was a crude and unprecise procedure and often accomplished in the field when felt the need was due. I had bent my TM1 barrel several times using the fork of a tree, above the hinge of a skeet house door, or sometimes just by several blows over a spare tire. On a Perazzi TM1, this required kinking of the solid rib. But you did what you had to do to achieve results. My idea was to have Tom build the new barrel bent upwards, then place the rib on it in such a way that the rib started out flat, then had a ¼" step-up about 14" from the muzzle. He spent many weeks on this project, and we shared numerous phone calls and ideas in the interim. He completed the barrel while I was attending the 1980 Alaska State Shoot. I was shooting well with the existing 34" barrel but decided to try the newly arrived 35" barrel for a 50-bird Jackpot Handicap held Sunday morning. The new barrel literally melted 50 targets and I knew I had found a new handicap weapon. The 35" barrel and mono-bloc were all Tom Seitz original, with the barrel threading into the monobloc as found in most rifles. Tom was quite proud of this and vowed never to make another like it; just too many hours involved.

A few years later, Tom and I both approved Seattle's premier gunsmith, Stan Baker, to duplicate the 35" barrel Tom had made for me. I believe Stan made a total of six of these to be fitted only to the Perazzi TM1. The only think I'm uncertain of is if the barrel is threaded or braised to the monobloc. I would assume braised. Stan's signature is engraved on the left side of the barrel just above the receiver, and my signature is engraved on the right side. I'm only aware of the location of one of these custom 35" barrels.

I can remember receiving the phone call from Larry Zerngast in October of 1988 as if it was yesterday. Larry had just talked to Tom's wife, Sue, and she was alarmed as Tom had been away elk hunting for several days and had not checked in with her as scheduled. Tom was planning to camp at an area that he could take the Revcon RV previously mentioned and use it as a base camp. His stepson and son-in-law had accompanied him. A day or so later, Larry called again with the tragic news. His son, Tommy, finally made the trip to find them as he knew where they would be camped. When he arrived at the site, he found Tom and the two others had subsided inside the RV. It was later determined that a ¼" bolt was missing between the cabin of the RV and the engine compartment. This type of RV required the engine running to produce hot water. It was determined the exhaust fan over the stove had been running and had drawn carbon monoxide into the living quarters with tragic results. The engine had quit running when it finally ran out of gas. It goes without saying, the trapshooting world lost a shining light never to be replaced.

LEO HARRISON III

When I first met Leo, it was probably around 1972 or 1973 at the Missouri State Shoot. He was still a skinny little kid at this point but could certainly point a Remington 1100 shotgun effectively. As I lived in the far western portion of Missouri and Leo was in the far eastern portion, we didn't cross paths all that many times until later years.

During the week of the Southern Grand held at the Silver Dollar Club in 1979, Britt Robinson and I ventured into St. Petersburg on a Thursday evening and found a terrific little country-western bar called the Rodeo. Lots of good music and a fun crowd. We had such a great time that evening that we decided to go back the next night and see if Big Leo would like to join us. He had just turned 21 a few months earlier and we thought he would enjoy the outing. This was a major understatement. Leo joined us Friday night. I can recall going out for a bit of two-step and returning to the table to find Leo holding a rum and coke, and a girl sitting on each knee. "I could get use to this" he said. He had an ear-to-ear grin I had never seen before. This was repeated Saturday evening and I have to say it appeared Leo thoroughly enjoyed himself. Driving out to the club Sunday morning, I saw Leo trudging along with his shaving kit headed towards the shower room. He was staying on the grounds in a friends RV. Head down and moving slowly, he looked a bit worn due the prior evening's activities, and if I recall correctly didn't shoot very well that weekend.

Later that same year, Leo, Martin Wilbur and I were shooting the Interstate shoot at Elliott's Shooting Park in Raytown, MO. While there, Missouri shooter Larry McKinley invited us to try our luck at spoonbill fishing on the Osage River below Truman Dam. I had never done this before, but since spoonbills (or paddlefish) were only found in this location and the Yangtze River in China, thought we should take advantage of this opportunity.

We arrived early in the morning and found Larry waiting for us, standing beside his Jon boat next to the tailwaters of the Osage River.

I thought this would be fun but soon discovered spoonbill fishing involves a tremendous amount of work. The procedure is to cast a 16-ounce lead weight combined with a large treble hook into the river; then use quick pumping motions while drifting downstream. All during this time you're reeling it back towards you with the hope of snagging one of these prehistoric monsters. Leo and Martin were both successful not long after we started, both landing fish in the 30 to 40-pound range. We toiled on, a total of 6 hours or so and I was ready to call it a day. The strength in my back and arms was completely gone and all of us were ready to go in. As I'm making my final reel-in, I strike something big, and it literally started dragging us all over the river. In fear of being pulled out of the boat, I had Martin hang onto me, and Leo hung onto Martin. After about 45 minutes of this, I finally get the fish up to the boat. A sixty-pounder snagged squarely in the fork of the tail. If Leo and Martin hadn't been there, I'm not sure what would have happened. This was my first, and last, venture for spoonbills, and I highly recommend you do not try this alone.

There was a period during the late 1970s that several of us became distracted by golf even though our principal purpose was trapshooting. There was a driving range and pro shop right across the road from Phoenix Trap & Skeet. I would go over and hit a bucket of balls now and then to kill time. Before long, Britt joined me, and eventually Leo. Leo became quite invested and even purchased a new set of clubs. I hate to admit it, but we started skipping 16-yard events to play golf. This was a common occurrence when in Phoenix, Tucson, Las Vegas, and sometimes Denver. John Hall and Dan Bonillas often joined the fray, and it's fair to say that all of us were quite amateur golfers.

Until 1982, the Sahara Hotel used to have its own course in Las Vegas, now re-named the Las Vegas National Golf Course. I had a great connection at the Sahara by the name of George Baxter. George was a pit boss and one of the best "people-people" I've ever met. We had shared time on houseboat fishing trips to Lake Powell on more than occasion and became very good friends. I called George one afternoon following a handicap event at the Mint Gun Club. We had finished shooting early and I had a foursome lined up for golf. George set everything up for me. When we arrived, two golf carts were reserved in my name; both with clubs as needed and each with a large cooler of iced down beverages. If I recall correctly, it was Britt, John, Leo and myself. Leo had just purchased his own clubs a week or two before and good shots off the tee were still uncommon. A 400-yard hole could easily become a 500-yard hole, but that was true for all of us.

We finally arrived at a par 3 hole that was 225 yards in length. Desert Inn Road ran parallel immediately to the north of this hole. This hole was also backed up a couple of groups when we arrived, so we took a short break until our time to tee up. When it was finally our turn, there was a couple of foursomes behind us that had caught up. When Leo hit his tee shot it was almost perfect, exactly the correct distance, but ended up in the sand trap just to the left of the green. He was extremely pleased with himself as it was a much better shot than any of our tee shots but unfortunately caught the sand. We moved down the fairway and began chipping up towards the green. Leo was last, leaning on his club and waiting in the sand for us to catch up. It was finally his turn, but he had never been in the sand before. We advised him of the proper protocol to the best of our limited knowledge. About 5 shots later, he was still in the sand and became very aggravated. He finally hauled off and kicked at the ball and ended up on his back in the sand. Keep in mind there were two groups at the tee box that witnessed all of this. Leo finally got up, picked up the ball and hurled it completely over Desert Inn Drive and stomped off to the next hole. In all my years around Leo at trapshooting events I had never seen him upset about anything. However, a few holes on the golf course revealed a previously unknown element of his personality!

During hunting season one fall, Leo drove over from Hannibal to Chillicothe, Missouri to shoot a few ducks and geese with me and my lifelong hunting and fishing buddy Emil Sechter. Our location was a field blind close to the Grand River and Fountain Grove Wildlife Area. The three of us and my black lab, Sam, entered the blind, with Leo sitting on the far-left side. I noticed immediately that even sitting down, the top of Leo's head protruded above the roof of the blind. He was wearing a brimmed camo hat so I placed a few more small branches with leaves around that end of the blind and decided he would be concealed adequately. Before long, a trio of Canada geese flew over and we managed to knock a couple of them down. My buddy and I left Leo in the blind while we retrieved the birds. While we were out amongst the decoys, several more geese departed the refuge and headed our way. Emil hollered over for Leo to get down. I just grinned and said- "He is down!"

Leo, travelling with his brother Scott, Martin Wilbur, accompanied by his girlfriend, and I in my own vehicle, caravanned to the Iowa State Shoot in 1981. Martin had a yellow Cadillac convertible at the time. It had a decent appearance but had a leak in the exhaust system and a slight emission problem. You could hear and see it coming from quite a distance. Leo and I pulled into a small Iowa town and stopped at a convenience store for fuel and snacks. We were about five minutes ahead of Martin. Leo and I were in paying the clerk when Martin rolled in. He rumbled up to the pump, then shut the Caddie down and emerged from the vehicle. Of course, the clerk had no idea this was the third leg of our group. Leo grinned and asked the clerk "I'll bet that's not who you expected to get out of that car is it?"

I rode home from Las Vegas with Leo following the chain of mid-winter western trapshooting events in 1979 or 1980. We stopped at a truck stop somewhere in Arizona for lunch and as we were paying our bill at the register, Leo noticed a counter display depicting the latest in fuzz buster technology. "I've been meaning to get one of these" and he went ahead and purchased the advertised "latest and greatest" in radar detection devices. We made it about 20 miles east on Interstate 40 before being pulled over and issued a speeding ticket.

Less than a month later, I was riding with him again after finishing the Southern Grand in Florida. We made it all the way to Illinois, then was pulled over again and issued another speeding ticket. After the State Trooper pulled away, we pulled back onto the Interstate. Without saying a word, the electric driver's side window suddenly rolled down and the fuzz buster went out the window.

At almost any gun club he visited, if he wasn't on the firing line you could find him inside the clubhouse at a card table. Leo loved playing 4-handed cutthroat Hearts, and he was very good at it. I'm sure I, along with many others, contributed to his travelling fund on many occasions.

Leo and I spent memorable time at Lake Creek, Alaska, fishing for King Salmon, and participated in one of the last true "Midnight Sun" trap tournaments in Fairbanks. Whatever the venue, having Leo along always made it more enjoyable.

I was blessed to have known Leo and I will always cherish the moments, and many laughs we shared. He was the true gentle giant in every way, on and off the trapshooting field.

LARRY GRAVESTOCK

I never had the pleasure of shooting on the same squad with Larry Gravestock as we hadn't crossed paths in the 1960s, and by the time I finished my military time and college he had practically retired as an active participant.

I remember reading about some of the scores he was registering from the 27-yard line that was unheard of during the late 1960s, early 1970s. And he did it consistently. His cumulative average on 24,000 handicap targets in 1972, '73 & '74 was over 93%. Most of these scores were with a pump gun and Larry shot at everything, in all conditions.

I had my first opportunity to watch him shoot at Elliott's Shooting Park during the annual Interstate Tournament in April of 1973. He had made the long drive from Texas to be there. Conditions were lousy, rainy and cool, but Larry was standing on the 27-yard line and center-punching one target after another using a Remington Model 31. Quick, smooth, with minimum gun movement and seemingly little effort. The barrel on the gun was bent upward in such a way that it was easily noticeable to onlookers. A couple of observers asked- "What the hell's the matter with that barrel"?

The other thing I noticed was how gently he closed the action of the gun. I discovered later that was necessary due to the extremely light trigger pull weight that he favored.

There were many interesting Gravestock stories circulating at the time, including about the car he drove. It was a full-sized Cadillac fitted with an extra fuel tank to add many miles of range. The purpose? Who knows, but this was a time of fuel shortages and increasing gasoline prices.

I can't recall who it was, it may have been Britt Robinson or Bill Dunlap, but they shared a story with me about Larry while at a tournament several years prior in Las Vegas. On a trip from the Mint Gun Club back to town, Larry asked his passengers how long they thought the broken white lines were that separated the lanes of the highway. There was a considerable number of estimates offered and finally some wagers were made. Larry pulled the car off the side of the road and jumped out with a tape measure. His guess was right on and he collected the money. A few days earlier while driving out to the club alone, he had already measured the lines in question!

I saw Larry briefly at the 1974 Grand. He was shooting a Perazzi Lusso grade TM1 single, barrel bent upward just like his Remington Model 31 predecessor. That following spring he hung it up, dropping out of trapshooting competition for many years.

Larry was to be inducted into the ATA Trapshooting Hall of Fame during the Grand American in 1987. This created quite a buzz as many believed he would enter a few events. That was not the case. He and his mother flew into Dayton Tuesday afternoon, attended the banquet and induction ceremony that evening, then departed just as suddenly.

In January 1990, I was behind the pro-shop counter making final preparations for the re-opening of the Las Vegas Gun Club to coincide with Valentine's Day. The phone rang and it was Larry Gravestock on the other end of the line. We exchanged some conversation and he finally said he was starting to shoot again and planned to attend our Midwinter Trapshooting Tournament coming up the end of February. He also asked if Bud Decot would be there as he needed fitting for a new pair of shooting glasses.

Sure enough, Larry came out for a few days of the tournament, entering in the 200 Singles Championship and three handicap events. He continued to shoot sparsely that spring and summer, including the Grand American.

He returned to Las Vegas the following year and entered the handicap events at our Midwinter Tournament in 1991. I also saw him at the California State Shoot in Kingsburg that summer. Following that, it appeared he retired from trapshooting once again.

On Christmas Eve 1991, I was wrapping things up around noon at the club and about to head home when Larry came through the front door. He said- "Hey Steve, I was just passing through and wanted to stop and say Merry Christmas!" He had another friend travelling with him. They stayed about thirty minutes and departed. I don't know where they had come from, or where they were going. That was the last time I ever saw him.

The last I heard of Larry was that he became a truck driver and living in California.

He was a wizard on the trap field and a pleasure to watch. I'm positive that he's the first person to ever bend a barrel for trapshooting. Britt Robinson confirmed that Larry bent a Remington Model 31 barrel for him at Amarillo in 1959.

He's the first person I'm aware of that really understood the benefit of vertically elevated patterns for success at long yardage. Many more would follow his example.

DON EWING

My earliest recollection of Don would have been at the Missouri State Shoot at Linn Creek in 1973. He drove a Dodge pick-up and was towing the largest 5th wheel trailer I had seen at that time. The rumor was that he had just recently won $105,000 at the crap tables while at the Golden West Grand in Reno. Supposedly he had an outboard motor and marine service shop in Onawa, IA, but I never knew him to spend any time there.

An extroverted personality if there ever was one, you couldn't help but immediately like Don Ewing. He had a loud and raucous voice & laughter that was infectious. He loved to play Hearts when not shooting and could always be found at one of the card tables between events, usually with Big Leo.

There were numerous stories that Don's mother had recently passed and left him in charge of six prime Iowa farm properties, apparently to the chagrin of some of his siblings.

During the 1975 Grand American I tied for the Clay Target Championship after a 22-way tie of 200s. The shoot-off was held over a period of two days and Don proved to be my biggest fan. Between rounds he would come up to me and ask if I needed a "sody pop" and continued to offer words of encouragement. He sat on the bench in front of the bleachers and watched every round, every target. When I finally emerged the victor, I don't believe there was anyone happier to see this than Don as he ran onto the field to offer congratulations. He appears in at least one of the Trap & Field photos that was taken capturing this moment.

I've always believed his huge win at the crap table mentioned above was the beginning of the end for Don Ewing. For years to follow, the excitement of that moment lead to a spiraling downturn that followed him for the rest of his life. Every subsequent trip to Las Vegas or Reno found Don trying to recapture the magic on the crap tables. It seemed that trapshooting became secondary to the gambling when in Nevada.

During a Las Vegas Fall Trapshooting Tournament, Don missed his first squad of one of the main handicaps due to a late departure from the casino. The hotel had sent him out to the gun club in one of their limos. He was able to catch his squad as they were starting their second trap and ran the last 75-straight. He then went to the practice trap and broke another 25 for the 100. This was a huge monetary gain as Las Vegas handicaps were still paying well at the time. Unfortunately, Mint Gun Club Manager, Gary Williams, disqualified the score as the program stated that missed squads would not be allowed to make up.

Over the next few years, Don Ewing stories were everywhere and becoming more bizarre. Family farms were being liquidated to support his gambling habits. His wife divorced him but managed to keep ownership of a small hotel they owned. Don was borrowing money from about anyone that would loan to him.

I'm not sure of the year, but it may have been 1982 or 1983. I had flown down from Anchorage to attend the Grand. Don was in poor financial condition by this time but showed up at the Grand, apparently with enough money to enter some of the events. He didn't have a gun, so Gene Sears loaned him a Perazzi TM1. At some point during the week, Don must have mentioned to one of his squad mates that he might consider selling the TM1 at the end of week. The squad mate was very interested and even gave Don a deposit on it. At the end of the week, Don sold the gun to someone else and disappeared.

I didn't see Don again until 1985. Alaska ATA State Delegate Maurice Oswald, Tom Sokol and I flew from Anchorage to Salt Lake City to attend the ATA Western Zone tournament at Larry Mitchell's club. It was our intent to bring the Western Zone to Alaska the following year; combined with the Alaska State Shoot. (We were successful and hosted the last non-telephonic ATA Western Zone shoot at the Birchwood facility in 1986.)

At the Salt Lake Gun Club, Don was working as a puller for the Western Zone tournament and living out of his black Buick Grand National. The current rumor was that he was in a tremendous amount of debt to a multitude of people around the country.

On Saturday evening of the tournament, a dinner and Special Event was being held in a banquet room of a nearby Holiday Inn. I asked Don if he would like to go and had him ride along with me. We re-lived some old times and shared some great conversations and laughter at the table that evening. He didn't appear to have a care in the world and just seemed to be the same old Don.

On the ride back to the gun club that evening, I asked him just how much he owed and if he had a way out. His response was not what I expected. "Stevie, just one good hour on the crap table and I would be debt-free." I had been around him very little for several years but now realized the full extent of his horrible addiction.

81

When we arrived back at the club, he got out of the car and asked if he might be able to borrow $100. I said no, but I'll give you a $100, which I did out of friendship. This would be the last time I would ever see him.

Shortly after leaving Alaska in 1987, Lidia and I were at Chuck and Loral I. Delaney's Game Fair in Anoka, MN. It was Labor Day weekend in September. Someone came up to me during the event and asked if I had heard about Don Ewing. I hadn't, and he went on to tell me that Don had been killed the day before. He had been visiting his daughter and son-in-law. After leaving their home, he struck an A-frame bridge on a country road travelling at a high rate of speed. It was believed he was killed instantly.

No matter what events may have preceded his death, Don was always a good friend to me. This was a sad and painful end to the story. I hope that it serves as a lesson learned to all those who read it.

At age 38, Don Ewing became the youngest shooter to enter Iowa's Trapshooting Hall of Fame in 1975

Dan Bonillas & John Hall- Fin, Fur, Feather & Clays

Dan Bonillas and I shot together for the first time in the 1973 Grand American Handicap, after having been placed on the same squad following the random squad drawings used for the main handicap events of those times. Beginning in 1976, Dan, John, & I would shoot together many times at the California State Shoot, the Golden West Grand, the Midwinter Tournaments at Phoenix, Tucson, Las Vegas, and of course the Grand American. There are just too many stories to even begin telling them all. The most memorable were probably those away from the trap fields.

The three of us, plus Gene Sears, Morris ("Morrie") Stinebring, and a few others I can't recall were part of the original Winchester Ammunition Advisory Board formed in 1975. We met with executives and representatives of the company once or twice each year to discuss product development, performance and trends in ammunition sales. These business meetings occurred at various locations, often including extracurricular activities such as hunting or fishing.

Our first assignment was for a successful launch of the new Winchester Super Target ammo. This was an all paper-hulled load manufactured to compete with the popular Federal paper shell. At the time, these were available at many of the local gun clubs, but no one was purchasing. Lloyd Pierce was vice-president of sales during this period and Ned Lilly was supervisor of trap and skeet promotions. I don't believe I've ever met two finer gentlemen.

One of our early meetings was at NILO Farms in East Alton, IL. NILO Farms became famous as a result of John Olin's National Champion Labrador Retriever, King Buck. Many dogs of several different hunting breeds were kenneled and trained there to support the hunting activities. Trap, Skeet, and Crazy Quail were available; sporting clays hadn't come around yet.

One of the most memorable moments of our trip occurred when Dan and I were sharing one of the duck blinds. We were located at the edge of a grove of trees at the base of a hill. There was a small lake behind us.

At this point I'll share what I learned about hunting ducks at NILO Farms.

When Mallard ducklings are old enough, a worker rounds them up in their pen and walks them from the top of the hill down to the lake below about 200 yards away. They spend some time swimming and splashing around in the lake, then they're walked back up the hill to the pens. Once they're old enough to fly, they're walked up an elevated plank in the pen until they come to the end which provides an opening. From that point they fly down to the lake. This process repeats itself over and over until they're fully conditioned.

When hunting season rolls around, at least three "hunting" blinds are between the pen and the lake. Dan and I were in one of these.

Mallards would fly over us on the way to the lake in groups of three or four. It was almost continuous shooting for 30 minutes or so. At some point I remember looking out of the blind and there was a single Mallard Drake walking down the trail right next to us. He cocked his head, quacked, and looked at us as he walked by. He wasn't about to fly.

The following fall, Winchester invited its advisory board members for a fishing trip to Quebec's Lac Desert as a kickoff event. This lake had a reputation for excellent smallmouth and pike fishing.

Everyone met in Hartford, CT, then boarded a chartered Falcon Fanjet to fly into Montreal. From there it was another chartered flight by float plane into Lac Desert.

The first morning out on the lake I was paired with Lloyd Pierce. We had a native guide running the boat which was equipped with a small outboard motor. The guide advised us of what lures to attach and we started trolling for pike immediately. The guide had to point at the preferred lures as we found out the only English word he apparently understood was "troll".

Within 15 minutes, I had a fish on. It turned out to be a Northern Pike in the 30-inch, 10-pound range. I brought it up to the boat and immediately released it. I assumed we were fishing for larger pike and there would be plenty of them. The guide yelled what I assumed was an obscenity and I thought he was going to jump in after the released fish. I didn't understand the concern until much later. That was the only fish I caught in three days, and one of the few fish caught on the entire trip. Fish would have to brought in from elsewhere for our shore lunches. I've never been on such a fish-less fishing trip. At the days end, everyone returned to the lodge and all fishing rods and gear were left on the closed-in front porch.

By the second morning there wasn't near as much enthusiasm to get up early and out on the lake. Several of us decided to have a good breakfast first. We went over to the kitchen/dining cabin and had one of the worst breakfasts possible. Soggy bacon and apparently powdered eggs. Even the toast was bad. How can you possibly operate a Canadian fishing resort without providing good fishing **or** good food?

Those that did go out early to fish that second morning were in for a surprise. During the night before, someone went out on the porch, ran several feet of line off each of the reels and cut it. The cut line was then reeled back on. The next morning, everyone's first cast resulted in their favorite lure being lost forever.

The lodge had a well-stocked bar that proved to be the most popular feature of the entire place, along with a large stone fireplace. We'd sit around in the evening sipping cocktails and sharing stories. One of the evening highlights was hearing Morrie scream while in the shower after someone had turned off his hot water.

After everyone had finally gone to bed, Ned Lilly would get back up a couple of times during the night and fix himself another drink or two. This happened the first two nights.

On the third night a trap was set.

The fireplace mantle was covered with adornments such as pewter candlesticks, platters & bowls. These could have been mistaken for old trapshooting trophies.

Everything was tied together with monofilament line. When Ned got up that night, he would walk into the line in the dim light and spring the trap.

For some unknown reason, Ned didn't get up that night.

We were all awoken at about daylight the next morning to a huge clatter in the main room and what appeared to be French swear words. One of our guides had come in to start the fireplace for us and became tangled up in the monofilament line. He didn't return and provide this service any of the following mornings.

Everyone returned home a day or two later. My claim to fame was that I caught the largest fish on the trip. Gene Sears caught at least one fish because I have a polaroid photo of it.

Regardless of the downsides, the trip certainly provided a lot of laughs. I wasn't directly involved in any of the mischievous pranks but I'm pretty sure I know who was.

I've made several trips in the fall to hunt California quail with Dan at his camp in the hills south of Livermore. A tremendous setting, with comfortable accommodations and a huge stone fireplace that dominated the main room. John Hall, Dan, and I spent many enjoyable evenings in that room following a day's hunting, appropriately accompanied by Jack Daniels and Dewar's White Label. Livermore trap shooter Don Hachmann was Dan's partner in the camp and hunted with us often, as did another one of Dan's friends, Ed Brandi. I was saddened to learn this cabin was lost recently in one of California's wildfires.

I've also made multiple trips over the years to hunt with John in Texas. His first camp was close to Pearsall, southwest of San Antonio. We'd spend the mornings spreading feed from a battery-powered device attached to the front of the jeep. We'd return later and find the quail close to the trail.

A few years later, John leased another place further south just west of Falfurrias. This area is referred to as the "sand pocket" country and produces a wealth of bobwhite. While there, John was asked by a friend in Houston, Harvey Houck, to be on the lookout for anything for sale in that area. John found a 3000-acre ranch for sale just a few miles west of his place. Harvey bought the ranch and built a gorgeous home on the property. It also had several outbuildings set up to comfortably accommodate guests.

During one of my visits, John and I had shot a bunch of quail one morning and were sitting back at camp having a few cocktails and relaxing. Harvey called and wanted to invite us to have dinner with him that evening. Neither of us had anything but hunting clothes with us, mostly which were covered with quail feathers and dog hair. Harvey insisted that we come. We finally said okay but you'll have to overlook our appearance and condition. John was about to hang up when Harvey added- "by the way, do you have any quail you can bring?"

It turned out that Harvey had invited four elderly couples to come down and spend a couple days with him at the ranch. Harvey took the fellas out for quail hunting during the day, loading them up into the back of the custom pick-up that was built just for this purpose. They'd follow the dogs around until they found some birds. Once the dogs were on point, Harvey would help them down from the pick-up to get into position. Unfortunately, by the time it took for all this to happen, the quail would run-off. The main course of the dinner that evening was supposed to be quail and Harvey & his buddies had produced only a single bird.

We showed up for dinner that evening and brought enough quail with us to easily feed 15-20 people. We turned these over to the cooks and servers and Harvey gave me a tour of the place.

Within the hour, Harvey's guests arrived from their remote accommodations on the property. These were all very elderly folks. I would guess that most of them were in their mid-80s. The ladies were all dressed to the max in their formal dresses and jewelry. I'm thinking what in the hell have we gotten ourselves into here. Their husbands were dressed to match, then there's John and I, fresh from the field and very much three sheets to the wind.

We had another cocktail or two before dinner (we were already well past our tipping point before we arrived) then were finally seated around the large dining room table.

Before long, table talk turned to hunting and shotguns.

Harvey asked me if I had to pick one gun for quail, what would it be? I think I mentioned a gun or two, but no strong preference. I wanted to keep my response short, trying not to slur my words.

Harvey was an extremely successful businessman in the steel industry, and I expected that he would prefer a high-grade Perazzi field gun, or perhaps an English side by side. Certainly nothing less than a Beretta SO series.

Instead, he went on to say he thought he might like to have a Beretta 686 or 687, but have it done with custom engraving and gold inlays.

John hadn't said a single word the entire time since we had been seated, and now, out of the blue, he blurts out- "Well Harvey, that would be just like dressing up an old gal."

Harvey had absolutely no response for such a comment and it became uncomfortably quiet around the table for several minutes to follow.

We managed to muddle our way through the rest of dinner, then got lost three times before finding our way back to John's place.

In the fall of 1980, Dan, John Hall, Dan's Uncle Danny, and I drew a party permit to hunt bull elk in the Jackson Hole Wyoming area. This was a late season permit that spanned a period a week before and a week after Thanksgiving.

Friends that we had made earlier at one of Bob Taylor's 50 Grand events at the Jackson Gun Club provided us with accommodations. Walker Cross was a partner in the local Holiday Inn that was managed by Tony Ligori. Both were long-time residents of Jackson. Walker and Tony had taken us out on Jackson Lake for Cutthroat Trout during a previous visit.

The day before the late season began, John and I took my Landcruiser and made a scouting trip up towards Yellowstone Park. Dan and his uncle went another direction.

There are two distinct elk herds that come into the National Elk Refuge each fall. One is the Teton herd; the other is the Yellowstone herd. The trick is to intercept them as they're making the annual migration.

While up in the Yellowstone area we encountered very heavy snow forcing us to use the bumper-mounted winch on one occasion. We didn't encounter any elk activity so returned to Jackson late that afternoon.

Just a few miles out of Jackson, with the Snake River bottom about a half mile off to our right, John suddenly says "What is that down there?"

I pulled off the road onto the shoulder and looked through my binoculars. The Snake River has heavy pine trees on both sides of it in this area.

There were elk coming through the pine trees into an open area on our side then turning south, apparently following a trail in the twilight.

I then noticed a huge herd of elk walking toward us in single file stretching from the mountainside across the river. The other amazing thing was that it appeared they were all mature bulls. This was obviously the migration of a portion of the Teton herd into the refuge. They would have to cross the road somewhere ahead of us to enter the refuge.

We pulled back onto the highway and hurried south. It was almost dark now. Finally, up ahead, we could see the elk in the road. We approached as close as we dared, pulled off onto the shoulder and turned off the engine.

For over an hour, we watched trophy bull after trophy bull cross the road in our headlights right in front of us. No spikes, cows, or calves amongst this group. For anyone that has ever enjoyed hunting elk, this was a show like no other.

We sipped on Dan's home-made peach brandy and enjoyed this lifetime event playing out right in front of us. This made the entire trip worthwhile.

Those having permits for the general area could attend drawings each morning inside the National Elk Refuge. You had to be present and sign up for the drawings. I believe they drew 10 names at around 5am. It seemed there were hundreds of hunters and guides there in the dark each morning. If drawn, there were limited areas on the north end of the refuge that could be hunted. There were also areas that were strictly prohibited. We knew there were a great number of bulls there; we had just seen them the evening before. Chances of being drawn were very slim. Incredibly, John was drawn the first morning we were there. We left him there and would pick him up at the end of the day. Dan, his uncle and I went on to hunt another area.

We had made another acquaintance during our stay in Jackson by the name of Bill Jett. Bill had been a big-game guide in Jackson for several years. He had friends in several areas along the Yellowstone elk herd migration route. They would inform Bill when they observed activity and we would intercept them along the way. Traditionally, the Yellowstone herd came in a few days following the Teton herd. No hurry, just a matter of time.

We returned to the refuge later that afternoon and found John. He was successful and had taken a nice bull. I can't remember exactly how we did it, but we moved the elk over to the Holiday Inn and hung it from the second- floor balcony for a couple of days. This was an entire field-dressed elk, not quartered, hanging by the hind legs, antlers on the ground. I'm positive this is the only Holiday Inn in the world you would be allowed to do such a thing.

A couple of days later, Dan was successful in the morning refuge drawing and killed a massive trophy bull.

That evening we were having dinner and a discussion arose on the proper bullet placement for elk. I was always an advocate of the shoulder shot, to break the animal down and assure success. Uncle Danny was a fierce advocate of the neck shot. I argued there was a tremendous amount of area in the neck that would not prove fatal. If you missed the spine, you'd likely lose the elk. This went back and forth awhile over several glasses of wine. I finally gave up.

John's hunt was completed so he left a couple of days later leaving the three of us there.

The following morning, Uncle Danny was successful in the morning drawing at the refuge. Dan and I dropped him off with his gear and would pick him up later in the day.

After a morning check-in with Bill Jett, we took another drive back up towards Yellowstone just in the event we might get lucky and see something. I still had a tag to fill. You didn't have to get too far out of the Jackson Hole area to notice the snow piled up in a hurry.

We headed back towards town early afternoon. As we were nearing Jackson, the refuge was now on our left.

Dan suddenly pulled off the road and said "Carmichael, look at that!" Off to our left, no more than 100 yards inside the refuge, was a huge bull elk bedded down under a tree. A true royal-plus bull, eight points on a side, just lying there with his head up. I pulled out my binoculars to have a closer look and it appeared he had a neck wound from the small amount of blood that was present. I remember thinking, "surely not."

We drove several more miles on around to the south and east side of the refuge to the area we had dropped off Uncle Danny.

When we found him, he was clearly beside himself; "Sonofabitch, you're not going to believe what happened. Huge, huge bull, I made a perfect shot and he ran off and crossed over into the restricted area. The rangers won't let me go get him. He's laying down right over there!"

I looked over and he was pointing right at the bull Dan and I had observed earlier from the highway on the west side of the refuge. He was further away now, but you could see he was still lying there with his head up.

I didn't say anything; Uncle Danny was already in enough pain.

It's true, or at least it was then. Any animal that made it into the restricted zone of the refuge could not be pursued. Nature would then take its course without further outside intervention.

I stayed a few more days in Jackson, still anticipating the Yellowstone elk herd's movement into the refuge.

The night before Thanksgiving, all the bars in town contributed to the annual Fireman's Ball. Drinks were free for the ladies, everyone else was $1. All proceeds were contributed to the fireman's fund. The turn-out was huge. I had no idea this many people even lived in the area. There were two main bars on the town square, the largest being the Million Dollar Cowboy Bar. The Silver Dollar was about a half block west of the square. The entire town square was packed all evening.

Right around the first of December I received a call at the motel room from Bill Jett. He had just been informed the entire Yellowstone elk herd had been trapped in Yellowstone Meadows for several days due to heavy snowfall. The Dubois Fire Department sent track vehicles and plows and cleared a trail for the herd to spend the winter just outside of Dubois. Obviously, they weren't coming to the refuge that winter.

This elk hunt was over. Uncle Danny and I didn't fill our tags but what a great trip.

Another elk hunting trip, fall 1981, I picked John up at the Denver airport and we travelled north to Ft. Collins to meet Jerry Walcott. Wayne Leslie was going to join us in a day or two along with Hugh Mchugh and his son Lance.

We left Ft. Collins and ventured west. Jerry drove a Class C bunkhouse model motorhome as far and high as he could go into the Rockies.

We ended up setting up camp just over ten thousand feet up, and in excellent hunting country. From this point we would take our Jeeps and 4-wheel drive vehicles.

We arrived late in the afternoon. After levelling the RV and arranging everything inside, it was time for relaxation and enjoying the scenery.

We had a few drinks, dinner, and shortly after retired for the evening.

I took the booth bed in the main cabin, and John took the bed over thc cab. Jerry took one of the four bunks in the back of the unit. He would be joined back there by the rest of the crew when they arrived.

After settling in, I was about to doze off, but kept hearing John flip-flopping around in his bed. Occasionally this flip-flopping would be accompanied by an extremely deep breath and almost gasping sounds. This went on for over 30 minutes and finally I asked him if he was okay. He responded- "I think I'm in serious trouble up here, can't relax or catch my breath." I reminded him he had travelled from sea level to over ten thousand feet in a few hours and hadn't adjusted to the thinner air yet.

"Thank God, I thought I was having a heart attack up here!" Within five minutes he was sound asleep.

Early one Spring, Dan mentioned that the area around his quail camp was having a ground squirrel population explosion and I should try to come over to help with eradication. I made the trip over in May.

The first morning out, we loaded up in a topless jeep armed with a scoped .222 and scoped .22 mag. We ended up parking under a large tree at the edge of huge open field.

We lowered the windshield and placed sandbags on the dash. He had brought a bottle of his home-made peach brandy along. Every kill resulted in a sip of the brandy.

We sat there and never moved all day. It was like an arcade. Squirrels would pop up, very similar to Prairie Dogs, anywhere from 50 to 450 yards. The distance of the target determined which rifle was used.

After about two hours, I lost Dan, now slumped over in the driver's seat. The brandy had taken its toll. I continued blazing on for another 4-5 hours and shot over 500 rounds of ammunition without him ever moving. At the time we left it didn't even appear we had made a dent in the squirrel population.

Prior to the winter chain in 1981, which included the Mint Gun Club's Mid-Winter Tournament, the Spring Grand in Phoenix, and finally back to Las Vegas for Bob Taylor's 100 Grand tournament, Dan had made two major trapshooting changes. These multiple tournaments would serve as the inauguration for both the custom Perazzi DB81 that had been made for him following his design input, plus the introduction of the all plastic and new-on-the-market Eclipse ammunition.

He would attempt to promote both products simultaneously through his established trapshooting prowess.

Things didn't go very well.

Dan started on his usual post 2, and I was starting on post 3 at the time. This put me in a position to closely observe every shot Dan made, and it wasn't pretty.

By the time we arrived at Bob Taylors I had witnessed two weeks of some of Dan's most dismal performances ever. This was highlighted by a lot of weird sounding ammunition, and it didn't make any difference if the empty hulls were red or green. It had gotten to the point I didn't know quite what to expect when he fired. It could be loud, quiet, or anything in between, and in many cases followed by a "lost" from the scorekeeper.

Everything culminated during one of the final handicaps at Bob Taylors.

We were on the last trap and Dan was performing sub-par as had been the case for the prior two weeks. He called for and went after the target only to hear a resounding "click" when he attempted to shoot. I looked over at him and he shook his head. This was a first as he hadn't experienced a total misfire up to this point. He opened the gun and the chamber was empty; he hadn't even loaded it. He told me later the empty chamber looked huge. A perfect ending to what must have seemed like three weeks of hell on the trap fields to one of the game's established premier performers.

Soon after, the DB81 and Eclipse ammunition both disappeared quietly, never to be seen again.

A Bit of
This & That

THE NEW, UNBREAKABLE, JOHN HALL 2-GUN CASE

At the 1975 Grand American in Vandalia, Texan John Hall was sitting at his vendor booth located approximately 100 yards west of the beer tent.

Back in these days, almost every vendor location at the Grand American was described by its proximity to the beer tent.

John had introduced his latest creation, the 2-gun molded plastic case; portable, affordable, and capable of protecting valuable firearms during commercial airline travel.

At the entry to John's vendor area was a large Elm tree and next to it an easel with a dry-erase board. On the board was written, "The new, unbreakable, John Hall 2-Gun Case, only $169.95."

Literally hundreds of visitors walked by the area, but not many inquiries about the new product.

One afternoon, Oklahoman Jim Kusel (nephew of Gene Sears) came sauntering by and stopped to visit with John and asked him about the new case. Jim was a big boy, and John came up with a marketing strategy to stimulate activity at the booth.

He asked Jim to take one of the cases on display and slam it into the Elm tree as hard as he possibly could.

After doubtfully questioning exactly what John was asking him to do, Jim did as he was told, hauled back and struck the tree with a mighty blow as many onlookers had stopped to see what the hell was going on.

Upon contact, the case exploded into dozens of pieces and Jim was standing there with only the handle in his hand and his jaw hanging down. John quietly took a drag off his Tiparillo, slowly stood up and walked over to the easel and board. He picked up an eraser, removed "unbreakable" from the sign and returned to his chair.

Regardless of the incident described above, the John Hall 2-gun case became extremely popular with trap shooters of this era.

John was an expert in plastic molding. I once visited his plant in Manvel, TX, and witnessed half-cases coming right out of the mold and being driven upon with a 3000 lb. forklift with no damage occurring. He told me later, however, that he struggled with the red cases. The drying agent used with the red dye often resulted in the red cases being too brittle. I should mention the red dye was the same as used in the popular Winchester AA hulls at that time.

John developed several products for the trapshooting market. First was the innovative plastic shell box carrier that you clipped onto your belt. This was followed by the All-American shooting shirts, and finally the Concentrator.

Not many were aware of the Concentrator as it never really caught on. Basically, it was a fold up visor with built in blinders that hung down on both sides, and a long bill providing the shooter with a sense of tunnel vision.

John first revealed this product to me in Phoenix during a clandestine meeting sitting in the front seat of my car. I didn't have to sign a non-disclosure form, but I was sworn to secrecy.

The potential popularity of the Concentrator suffered a setback at the 1979 Grand during one of the early handicaps.

Missouri shooter Phil Matthews was leading our squad, was down several targets, and decided he would give the new device a try on our last trap. Dan Bonillas was on post 2, I was on post 3, John Hall on post 4, and Neal Crausbay on post 5.

Phil commenced to shoot a "zero" on his first post and that's pretty much the story of the beginning, and the end, of the Concentrator. Neal didn't fare much better as he fired a "1" on his first post and was heard telling Phil as he passed by on his walk to post one "I kicked your ass!"

I mentioned earlier that John would join us for an outing of golf now and then.

Mike Jordan, long-time Winchester rep, John and I would occasionally play at the Vandalia course during the Grand American.

On one of these ventures we arrived at the course and John was still in his cowboy boots. I had a brand-new pair of Adidas tennis shoes still in the box. Though John is three inches taller than me, my feet are two sizes larger than his. I offered him the shoes which he gladly accepted.

I should add that Mike Jordan is an excellent golfer; John & I, not so much. We finally came to a hole where John hooked his tee shot a bit and it disappeared into a swampy area left of the fairway. I ended up on the right portion of the fairway and Mike was right down the middle.

We moved forwards for our second shots. While I'm waiting to hit, I'm watching John over in the high grass looking for his ball. I walked over to help him. At about the time I got there he had found it and hollered "It's playable!"

I looked and he was squaring up his club face to the ball while standing in ankle-deep water, still wearing my brand new shoes.

I've made several trips to south Texas over the past years to enjoy time with John and hunt quail. On one of these trips, I flew commercial into Houston, then John and I flew down to his ranch in his Cessna 210.

He had a makeshift landing area along one of the fence lines bordering the property. The wind was blowing slightly when we touched down. We bounced back in the air, touched down again, and repeated this twice more.

Finally, we settled in and taxied up to a barn and the waiting pick-up truck. John looked over at me, grinned, and said "That was three of the best landings I've ever made!"

At some point during the mid to late 80s, John declared he would no longer be shooting at anything as the result of calling "Pull" and has been true to his word ever since. He spends most of his time now enjoying his ranch in superb quail country just west of Falfurrias, TX.

THE OPPOSITE OF NIGHT SHOOTING

On Wednesday, of Bob Taylors 1977 "100 Grand" program, I woke up at the Sahara Hotel, and turned on the TV to find out the town had been blanketed in snow overnight.

I threw open the heavy drapes concealing the window and sure enough, it was bright out there. It was January 31st, and snow does occasionally fall in Las Vegas during the winter months, but usually a lesser amount that melts off quickly. The town was completely paralyzed with hardly any traffic moving at all as there are no snowplows in Las Vegas.

When I arrived at the club, they were dealing with removing the 7" snowfall from the walkways and preparing to start the 16-yard event. It wasn't all that cold and was dead-calm, truly an unusual set of conditions for Las Vegas.

Our squad was comprised of Dan Orlich on post 1, Dan Bonillas on post 2, I was on post 3, John Hall on post 4, and Britt Robinson on post 5. When we took the line, we were all amazed at what we were seeing.

Literally everything in front of us was pure white. The ground, the trap house, and everything in the background including the Sheep Mountain Range eight miles away.

Orlich asked if everyone was ready, then asked for the traditional "Let's see one." The solid black target looked like a beach ball just hanging out there. I thought this is really going to be fun.

We were about to commence shooting, when out of the blue John quips "Hey, is this the opposite of night shooting?"

It did appear so. After a few comments and snickers we proceeded. As it turned out, none of us broke the 100. It seemed the total lack of perspective had taken its toll.

TOOLS & TRICKS OF THE TRADE

For many years the guns I used for trapshooting would have been considered standard. There was nothing special about the Model 12 used in my early years other than I replaced the straight trap stock with a Monte Carlo that one of my uncles made for me in his basement. The new stock was first fitted with a green Jenkins pad, and eventually a curved, adjustable Morgan pad.

Not long after installing the Morgan pad, I was competing as a Junior at the 1966 Grand American. While shooting a preliminary weekend 16yd event I started feeling pain in my shoulder. I rounded off one the tips of the recoil pad believing this was the source of the problem. The pain continued in the next event and had intensified by the time I finished. I was in serious trouble as this was just the preliminaries and I was facing six main days on the horizon. I discussed this dilemma with my parents and agreed something needed to be done. We decided to visit Jesse Edwards and check out the new Edwards Recoil Reducer which was making its Grand American debut.

After receiving a brief description of the benefits of the new device, I left the gun with Jesse for the installation. After the job was completed, I made a visit to the practice traps to test it out. I couldn't believe the difference. My Grand had been salvaged.

I went back to Jesse's vendor site and praised him and his product. He took me aside and said "I have to share something with you. When I was removing the Morgan pad, I discovered the small top screw in the pad had backed out to the point it was almost exposed. Every time you fired the top of that screw was repeatedly hitting you in same exact spot creating a hammer & punch effect!" Ouch. Well, that certainly explained the intensity of the pain.

The next day my dad and I teamed up to win the Father & Son Championship while I also took high Junior. Two days later I was the Junior Clay Target Champion. Obviously, I couldn't say enough good things about Jesse Edwards. Had I not requested his services my 1966 Grand American would have had entirely different results.

Over the years I experimented with a variety of different recoil-reducing devices. Wayne Leslie and Ray Stafford introduced the 2R device in the 70s, as did Louis Hutchison with Hiram's Beartrap. Later, Steve Jones of CA developed the Dead Mule. Some devices used mercury, some used mechanical springs, and some used hydraulic flood forced through baffles. All seemed to work reasonably well. How much is actually attributed to simply weight vs function has been discussed and debated among shooters for decades.

While I always respected my equipment, how well it performed for me was much more important than how it looked. I had no problem taking a rasp to a stock in the middle of a tournament if it provided the results I was looking for. In the mid-70s, adjustable stocks had not yet hit the scene.

Same for adjustable point of impact. On more than one occasion I bent the barrel up on my TM1 during a tournament. This was an ugly process with less than finite results. Plus, it kinked the solid rib.

Many were appalled by the process being applied to a high-quality firearm, but long as I achieved the needed results I really didn't care. It worked for me.

Close observation had proved to me that more handicap targets were shot under than any other location. Many shooters were working with only the top half of their pattern at best. If you doubt this, watch the scores tank during a strong headwind and rising targets. I always favored working with the bottom half of the pattern. If you shot quickly as I did, the target was always raising.

At Bob Taylor's 1978 Midwinter Tournament, I spent the first four days struggling with handicap. I hadn't performed very well at Phoenix the week before and had about convinced myself it was time for a point of impact adjustment. The tell-tale sign for me was always the same. If I was having problems with right angles, it was time for an upward adjustment (I'm left-handed).

On Friday afternoons handicap, I missed two on each of the first two fields.

We arrived at the third field and it was backed up a squad. I decided now was the time.

I took my TM1 apart, handed the forearm to John, and took the barrel over to one of the temporary skeet houses that had been pulled off the line into the parking lot during the trap tournament.

I opened the skeet house door, placed the barrel in the gap right above the hinge, and applied pressure. Since the barrel had been bent previously and the already rib kinked, it didn't take very long to achieve the results I wanted.

Once satisfied, I returned to the field and reassembled the gun, now with a hint of green paint on the rib where it had contacted the skeet house.

I broke the last 50 for a 96. The next handicap the following morning I managed a 97.

For the three days prior to this, a well-dressed elderly gentleman had followed our squad down the line and watched us. He never approached any of us or spoke; just observed. When we finished a round and were coming off the line, he would get up and move on down to the next field and have a seat on a bench.

We were halfway through Sunday's handicap and I hadn't noticed him following us that morning.

When we arrived at our third field and were placing our guns in the rack, John nudged me and said "Get a load of this" while pointing over to the skeet house I had visited a couple of days before.

The old gentleman that had been watching us was now bending barrels for fellow shooters! There were three people in line, barrels in hand. It appeared they were giving him $20 per pop. Truly amazing!

I've always considered the trigger mechanism to be one of the most critical factors of any tournament gun, especially after what happened at the 1978 Grand American.

I had been shooting well all year then took a nosedive that started with the 200 singles on Monday. After breaking the morning 100, I started to struggle in the afternoon and eventually lost two targets.

The next day I performed poorly in the handicap, then a complete disaster in Wednesday's Clay Target Championship.

Everyone else was shooting well on the squad around me and I was completely baffled. Something felt physically wrong, and I couldn't put my finger on it. I almost felt like I was flinching, but sporadically, and with no warning.

After finishing Wednesday's singles championship, I decided to take my gun to Giacomo Arrighini. Perazzi's master gunsmith was still located in the back of the old Ithaca building at that time.

I routinely had my hammer springs replaced at the Grand, plus had the trigger/sear engagement checked. This year was no exception as I had this service done on preliminary Thursday. I explained what had been happening and left the gun with him.

A couple of hours later I was in the grandstand area waiting for the Clay Target Championship shoot-offs to begin when Giacomo found me. He asked me to come back to the shop with him so he could show me what he had discovered.

He had taken the trigger out of the gun and secured it in a vice. He cocked it, then placed the trigger pull gauge on it and fired. It was about 30 ounces which was normal for me. He held his finger up apprehensively and said wait and watch. He repeated this process about twenty times which revealed the pull weight varying from under 12 ounces to over 80 ounces.

I had started my week off with my usual routine trigger maintenance, so what had happened? Giacomo had figured it out. He discovered one of the holes in the trigger frame had wallowed out and was egg-shaped. Apparently, the steel in the frame had not been properly hardened. The stainless-steel pin that held the hammer/sear assembly in place had created the damage after thousands of rounds. Giacomo stated he had never seen this happen before.

He fitted a completely new trigger and the problem was solved. To this day, I have never heard of another single shooter having a Perazzi trigger frame failure.

After I returned home from the Grand, I gave Tom Seitz a call and shared the story with him. I wanted to make sure I didn't have a repeat experience down the road and would like to do anything possible as preventive maintenance.

Tom asked me to send him the new trigger once I had completed my season. He would make a modification that may prove to be helpful.

A couple of months later I would be finished competing for a while, following the completion of the Missouri Fall Handicap. I pulled the trigger out, packaged it up and sent it off to Tom.

A couple of weeks later he called and said it was on the way back to me, and to give him a call once it arrived so we could discuss it.

I received the trigger a couple of days later, opened it up and called Tom.

He told me to look for the small black bolt that had been installed in the back of the sear. By turning the bolt one way or the other with a small Allen wrench, I could adjust the pull weight from 28-ounce to 40-ounce, and it would remain at that weight. He also had me take a close look at the hammer. It was almost invisible, but I could barely see something different in the top of the hammer. He explained that he had drilled down into the top of the hammer and inserted a stainless-steel pin that extended into the arc of the hammer. The arc of the hammer was the location where Perazzi hammers would eventually break after thousands of rounds. It would start with a slight crack, then get worse until complete failure if not replaced. Once the top of the hammer and pin had been polished off you couldn't even tell it was there. He had also re-hardened the frame. Tom had built an almost completely fool-proof trigger for me that served me well for many years.

Once again, the genius of Tom Seitz had come to surface. I was never without a trigger gauge after my Grand debacle. I routinely checked my trigger pull weights before every event for the remainder of my shooting career.

Following the development of fully adjustable stocks, I can't imagine any quality tournament trap grade gun not having one. The difference in fitting correctly and almost fitting correctly for handicap trapshooting is massive.

When the Stice adjustable comb came along in 1978, I was probably one of the first customers. The patented, early adjustable combs produced by Clyde Stice were either right or left-handed based on location of the adjusting screws. These early combs were only adjustable up and down, but a huge milestone in the refinement of trapshooting equipment. These obviously lead to the fully adjustable stocks of today which are now a standard in the industry.

I worked closely with Fred Wenig and Reinhart Fajen to refine this product in the summer of 1980 and won my third Grand American All-Around Championship using the prototype. This win followed a shoot-off in front of a grandstand full of onlookers who were curious about the new stock.

A month later I was fishing in Alaska and staying at the home of Jerry and Donna Urling in Anchorage. During a call home, I received the news that Fred Wenig needed me to call him as soon as possible.

I checked in with Fred the next day and he explained they needed a photograph of the stock for the new Fajen catalog. It was urgent as they were facing a deadline for publication and I had the only Fajen Adjustable Trap Stock in existence.

As usual during my trips to Alaska, I had my Canon AE-1 camera along with me and set up a temporary studio in Jerry and Donna's garage. The receiver of the gun was placed on a counter covered with a white sheet, and I took a series of photos from the top of a step ladder looking down.

The next day I found a photo shop that developed what I needed. I express mailed these back to Missouri and made the deadline. This photo of the new Adjustable Trap Stock, taken in a garage, was used, and appeared in the Fajen catalog for many years thereafter.

I had a definite preference of recoil pads. My all-time favorite was the Pachmayr Old English combined with zero pitch. This is a flat pad that is not too firm nor soft; just right. Pads that are too soft allow excessive gun movement and felt recoil to the cheek. I mounted the gun high on my shoulder so preferred to round the bottom of the pad just a bit to keep it from hanging up when mounting. I had no use for some of the tackier pads that came along in more recent years. They would hang up on my shirt and create disruption in timing and need for re-mounting. I tried to avoid that at all costs. I think every shooter has a personal timing & flow that's important to consistently achieve good results.

An area of importance that may be overlooked by many shooters is the stock grip. To me this is another one of the critical areas. Your grip on the stock provides the primary control of the gun; at least in 16yd and handicap shooting. I learned early on that more downturn in a stock grip resulted in creating a void in the palm of your hand. At least this was the case for me.

In some of my early work with Reinhart Fajen in the late 1970s, we experimented a great deal with this while developing the Adjustable Trap Stock. The correct amount of downturn combined with the correct amount of palm swell proved to be the right combination allowing 100% contact with your palm. My best results were when the stock grip pressure was about double the fore end grip pressure. At this point precise control of gun movement was achieved.

Like most trap shooters of the 1960s, many hours were spent on a reloader. A Junior model from C & R Specialties to be exact. If you were concentrating, you could produce about 125 round/hour, but you really had to be moving.

Red Dot powder could be purchased by the pound in a brown paper bag at the gun club, and shot was $4.25/25# bag. A box of reloaded shells came in at about 90 cents. (a round of 25 practice targets was only 50 cents!)

After I returned home from the military, I graduated to a Texan reloader but could never reproduce a load I was satisfied with on long yardage.

Everyone develops ammunition preferences and I've run the full gamut on this. I believe the majority of my seven 100 straights from 27 yards were achieved with 2 3/4 dram, 1 1/8 ounce 8's. At one point I decided 7 ½ shot might perform better with less pattern drift in strong winds and went with that. I've also performed well with standard 3 dram 7 1/2s so I would recommend whatever satisfies you mentally. The most important factor for me was consistency of the load.

However, I've never been a personal fan of Handicap, Super Handicap or Nitros. These are high quality and extremely consistent but combined with 1 1/8 ounce of shot resulted in excessive recoil for me. I could make it through the first box or two without incident but would eventually find myself coming out of the gun.

I'm sure at least some of you reading this remember the Remington targets that were used at the 1998, 1999, and 2000 Grand American.

There were numerous complaints on the hardness of the targets due to all the dusted targets that were observed.

My own opinion was the targets were too soft, not hard, allowing them to be penetrated without shattering. At any rate, my squad mates experienced problems; all using either Super Handicap or Nitro loads, and all dusting many targets. I stayed with light 7 1/2s and had at least one good handicap each of these years and never experienced a problem with dusted targets. It was my belief the light loads patterned a little tighter and placed more shot on the targets. Maybe yes, maybe no. It's what I believed and that's at least half the battle.

THE "F" WORD

The dreaded "F" word in trapshooting can only be one thing-"flinch". At some point in their career, almost every trap shooter deals with this in some form or another. Mine came when least expected.

I was shooting a doubles event at the Arizona State Shoot at the Phoenix Trap & Skeet Club. It was March 1976.

Everything was going along just fine, then it hit. My pair came out as called for and I made my normal movement at the first target. Nothing happened. I lowered the gun but didn't open it. Back in those days opening it would result in immediate lost pair.

David Bopp was on the squad and looked over and asked what happened. I told him I had no idea. I brought the gun back up to my shoulder and fired off both rounds so it was lost-a-pair anyway. This happened a couple of more times before the round was finished.

I was totally perplexed and tried to determine what might have led up to this.

A couple of days before this happened, I had the second barrel trigger lightened a bit. I also was not well rested the day this occurred, and it was the third event of a long day. I decided it may have been a combination of these two things.

I had the trigger reset to its original pull weight and figured that would be the end of it.

I couldn't have been more incorrect.

This was just the start of an affliction that plagued me through spring and summer and occurred only on the first bird of doubles. This was occurring at a rate of about 5 times per 100 targets. You never knew when it was going to strike. You could get comfortable for a few pair, then wham.

I had many scores in the low 90s that spring and summer. I became reasonably adept at breaking both targets on the way down, just feet above the ground. I put off considering a release trigger as my 16 yard and handicap shooting was good and apparently unaffected.

The Grand American rolled around in August and the flinching continued in both preliminary double's events.

I broke 200 in the Monday singles race, and 95 in Tuesday's handicap. I was off to a decent start in the High-Over-All, but now had to deal with Tuesday's doubles race and I'm dreading it.

About an hour before our squad is due to take the line for the Class Doubles, I decided to pay Giacomo another visit.

When I arrived at the shop, California shooter Don Slavich was also there. I told Giacomo what I had been struggling with, for how long, and was ready to take the plunge and try a release. He and Don were both a bit amazed.

Now, during the Grand American? I stated I had absolutely nothing to lose and 30 minutes to practice with it before our squad was up.

Giacomo recommended a release-pull trigger since I wasn't flinching on the second target. He pulled out a new release/pull trigger that was actually in a factory Perazzi trigger box. With very minor adjustments, he fitted the new trigger and I was off to the practice traps. Don said he needed to see this and accompanied me.

I purchased two, 12-pair practice tickets.

On the first round I missed the first 4 or 5 pair. It was awful. I was used to mounting the gun and calling quickly. I now had this whole new separate step in the process that was throwing everything off.

I quickly decided I needed to be setting the trigger at the same time I was finalizing the mount, eliminating the extra step and re-establishing the timing I was accustomed to. Once I did that, I broke the last 5 or 6 pair of the first round, then, broke all 12 pair of the second round.

I felt more comfortable with doubles than I had felt for the past 4 months.

I made it in time to shoot the event and broke a 98, with no effort or panic. I broke a 97 later in the main race but my sanity had been restored.

I stayed with the release/pull trigger for doubles for the rest of my shooting career.

I didn't experience a flinch on 16 yard or handicap until much later. In 2005, I had taken my son to San Antonio for the Southwest Grand. He was my main motivating factor for shooting during this period and I enjoyed spending the time with him.

I was using a TS2000 I had acquired from Tony DeSimone and was shooting in one of the early handicap events when it hit.

Springtime in San Antonio always seems to produce winds coming out of the southeast at some point during the week. Probably a result of a nearby thunderstorm or activity in the Gulf of Mexico. These conditions usually result is a climbing right-hand and diving left-hand target.

Normally, prevailing winds in the western part of the United States cause the targets to do the opposite, i.e., low right-high left.

I wasn't used to chasing left angles downhill and eventually flinched on one. This was bad news as I was well-aware once the seed was planted it always seemed to be there.

Sure enough, not long after that, I experienced another flinch and accepted the fact I was on my way to a release trigger for 16 yard and handicap as well.

I made the complete crossover a few weeks later and continued with the release from that point forward. I didn't find it difficult at all, but this was late in my shooting career and my emphasis was not at all on winning as it had been many years before.

If you must go to a release to continue enjoying shooting, then by all means, do so. However, I advise you to make every effort to obtain the very best release trigger possible. This is not an area to cut corners.

I've heard of a few rare cases of individuals being able to wean themselves off release triggers and return to pull triggers without continued flinching. I would have tried this if I was still competing seriously. There are simply fewer moving parts in a pull trigger and less likelihood of something going wrong.

COACHING

In 1976, Texan John Hall formed "All American Shooting Clinics" and asked Dan Bonillas and I to join him in offering travelling trapshooting clinics to different parts of the country.

At the time, there wasn't anyone offering this type of service.

Our first class was at Bob Taylor's Trapshooting Country Club in Las Vegas, May1977. We accepted a maximum of 30 students and broke them down into three groups of 10.

Over a period of three days, each of us worked with a group; John specializing in doubles, Dan in handicap, and I handled the 16-yard portion.

Before undertaking the first class, I realized I had never really thought about how I approached trapshooting, I just did it. Now I was going to have to convey this to others, which would require my own self-analysis.

The first class was a success, and we followed up with a second class in Orlando, Florida.

Following the second class, I met with John and Dan to discuss the future of this endeavor. I felt that 10 shooters in a single day was beyond my ability to achieve maximum results with the students.

At this point we went our own separate ways regarding teaching, and I found I was much happier with a maximum of 5 students per day, and 2-3 was even better. The issue was not with new students, but rather with the more experienced. I felt it necessary to watch many rounds over the shoulder of an accomplished AA shooter to discover what may take him/her to the next level.

One question I've been asked many, many times. "What is the most common miss?" Without hesitation, when referring to a right-hand hand shooter with both eyes open, I've observed the pattern to always be low and left of center on the target, regardless of angle. This has proved to be universal.

In 2000, Bob Schultz and I travelled to New Zealand to conduct clinics at gun clubs in Auckland, Christchurch, and Hamilton.

The "Down the Line" game popular in this part of the world is quite similar to our own 16-yard game, but slightly wider angles, a bit more target speed, and the shooter is allowed two shots. We worked with 10 shooters in each class and determined that all except one used both eyes while shooting.

By the time we reached our final clinic in Hamilton, we had named a reoccurring phenomenon we had observed over and over as the Eight O'clock Syndrome.

All 20 shooters at the first two clinics exhibited this. The vast majority of their patterns were low and to the left of the target, even when they were successful breaking the target.

At the final class, only 9 of the shooters were low and left, and one was just low. He was the lone one-eyed shooter, proving to me that binocular vision has a left-right effect on patterns and point of impact regardless of master eye.

I had the opportunity to coach both of my children at an early age; daughter Fabriana, and son, Stef.

Both grew up in the Las Vegas clubhouse and eventually competed along with almost 60 other kids in a Tuesday night .410 league created for youngsters and their parents in 1996. At the time they would have been 7 and 5 respectively.

Fabriana became an excellent trap shooter and competed with an all-girls team ("TLC" aka Trap Lovin' Chicks) in our Wednesday night trap league for many years, though she never had much interest in registered targets.

Stef also competed in league and went on to enter ATA shooting at the age of 9. As a youngster in grade school, he was usually the smallest in his class but made up for this in sheer determination.

By the age of 10 he was handling a cut down BT99 with no problem, but we hadn't tackled doubles yet. Due to his size I wasn't sure if he could handle the speed of movement necessary to be successful at doubles.

During the summer months he would often hang out with me at the clubhouse.

One day I noticed he was watching a video on the pro shop's computer monitor. He would sit there for extended periods and practice at the doubles portion of a DVD titled "Sportsman's Challenge", distributed by Cabela's in 1998. The DVD presented very adequate graphics illustrating trap, skeet, sporting clays, and trap doubles. The computer mouse was used to place the virtual gun barrel over the trap house. You then clicked the mouse to release the target, then click again to shoot.

Stef became extremely proficient at breaking the virtual doubles quickly and consistently. He also learned the faster he could break the first target resulted in a shorter and easier move to the second one. This went on for weeks as he developed a keen sense of timing combined with where to hold, and pair after pair of successful shots. He made the game appear extremely easy, but my own attempts proved differently.

One day I told him it may be time to try the real thing. One of our club rental guns was a Beretta 302 with 28" barrel and stock cut down to about 14". He could handle this comfortably, so we used it for his first doubles attempt.

I was amazed at what transpired.

Right from the beginning, pair after pair of centered hits, quickly and smoothly. His hold, timing and proficiency were identical to had I had observed while viewing his interaction with the DVD. He broke pair after pair, effortlessly, quickly, and dead center using the same methods he had developed on a video game. He was following the same timing he had learned on a video game.

Stef went on to become an excellent ATA doubles competitor. At the age of 13, he broke his first 100 in doubles at the Missouri Fall Handicap and shot off with Kay Ohye. Three weeks later, he broke his second 100 in doubles at Tucson's Autumn Grand and shot-off with Harlan Campbell.

He would later be selected as Captain of the 2006 All-American team for sub-juniors.

While I would like to take credit for his doubles prowess, I must defer to "Sportsman's Challenge" and have recommended this DVD as a training tool to several shooters that have struggled with proficiency in doubles.

Obviously, there's no magic here, but this may help the average doubles shooter to move forward in the right direction. Doubles is not simply one shot followed by another. Unique timing is established for both shots, unlike any other shot made on a 16 yard or handicap target.

Doubles consistency came late for me after determining exactly how I needed the gun set up, then burning thousands of targets. To me, the key was always taking the first target quickly and with minimal barrel movement. If you're not moving upward at the second target, you're probably taking the first target too late.

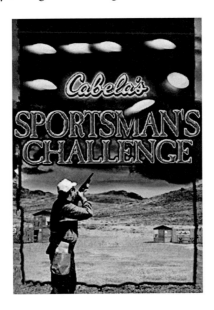

TRAP HELP

Stories about trap help deserve their own special place, not only from a competitor's perspective but also as a club operator. Some of the things experienced and witnessed would be unbelievable had I not experienced it first-hand.

Being a trap worker was a considerably more difficult job prior to the turn of the last century. Automatic traps were still new on the scene, plus under a considerable amount of scrutiny, and voice release systems were unheard of.

Every clay target had to be placed on a mechanical throwing arm by someone sitting in the very limited confines of the trap house, often for hours on end.

Every target had to be released at the shooter's command by someone pushing a button on the end of a cord while simultaneously scoring!

Ironically, some of the richest trapshooting tournaments in the country were at the mercy of trap help with little or no experience. This was truly a conundrum.

Mid-winter tournaments in Tucson, Phoenix, or Las Vegas were often held during a time of year that high school and college students were unavailable. This often led to procuring warm bodies from about any source available.

And, it took a lot of bodies when you considered full staffing. For each four traps, we hired five scorekeepers and five loaders. All machines in the trap house were handset at the time. This allowed for a "relief crew" for each four traps.

Crews were hired from multiple agencies and training periods were usually set up the weekend before the tournament. A normal procedure used at the Las Vegas Gun Club (formerly the "Sahara" and "Mint Gun Club") offered shooters practice at half-price to assure enough activity to train both scorekeepers and target setters.

Unfortunately, when work crews arrived each morning of the tournament, some were inevitably untrained replacements. This occurred daily and was the most difficult aspect of conducting a major trapshooting tournament during the winter months.

As the tournament host, I was never comfortable with how things were going until the last shot had been fired.

A few extraordinary trap help occurrences that come to mind:

- A puller/scorekeeper once burst into flames at the Las Vegas Gun Club. We were changing posts during a handicap event and the scorekeeper was calling out the scores. Suddenly, he jumped down from the scorer's elevated chair screaming. Apparently, he had been smoking and a hot ash worked its way into the sleeve of his windbreaker. The ash began to smolder, then subsequently broke out into flames. We rolled him around on the ground until extinguished. He was very lucky, only minor burns to one arm and complete loss of a windbreaker.

- Our squad was approaching the third field during a handicap event at Bob Taylor's 1976 January tournament. It was cold and blustery. We didn't see any trap help around until the doors of an old pick-up truck in the parking lot opened up. A guy, a girl, and a Labrador Retriever emerged. The girl was the scorekeeper, and the guy and the dog both disappeared inside the trap house. Gene Sears was on the squad and said jokingly "I don't care which one, but one of them needs to come out of that trap house." Sure enough, our scorekeeper saunters out to the trap house, peaks around the corner and says "Hey, a guy back there says he doesn't care which one, but one of you need to come out of there right now!" A couple of minutes later the Labrador emerged and we proceeded with the round.

- At the Mint Gun Club during a handicap event, Britt Robinson was on post 5 of our squad and having difficulty with the pulls. Britt called softly and any wind at all worked against him. Finally, he hollers over to the scorekeeper; a teenage girl leaning back in her folding chair with her shades on, twirling the release button on the end of the cord. "Miss, can you hear me OK?" She responds- "I can hear you just fine." She proceeded to give him three additional slow pulls of which he missed two. Britt didn't say anything, but I could hear him behind me noticeably stomping from post 5 to 1 while she glared at him and loudly called out scores of "5, 5, 5, 5 & 3", with emphasis on the 3!

- We're on the last round of a handicap event at Sage Hill's Golden West Grand on one of the lower trap fields to the west of the clubhouse. The ground terraced off drastically immediately behind the 27-yard walkways. The scorekeeper was sitting in a folding chair right on the edge of the drop-off between station 2 and 3. I noticed him leaning back on the rear two legs of the chair while we were changing posts as he was calling out our scores. We completed a couple of posts without

131

incident when suddenly we hear a scream and the scorekeeper is rolling down the hill behind us. To make matters worse, he still had the head of the pull cord in his hand with the release button, pulling it right off the end of the cord. They sent in a relief scorekeeper, but we had to wait until someone showed up with a new pull cord before we could finish the round.

- During a Mid-Winter tournament in Las Vegas, a squad took the firing line and the squad leader asked to see a target. The red flag had been lowered, but no targets are coming out. After repeated failed attempts, Chuck Elton of Golden West Industries was called by radio to the field. (GWI provided traps for major tournaments in the West for many years) Chuck walked out the left side of the trap house and peered inside. He shook his head, looked back at us and stated- "You're not going to believe this?" The target setter had unplugged the trap and plugged in his electric skillet to fry up some chicken!

- About three days into a major event in Las Vegas, I received a dreaded call on the 2-way radio from a Line Referee. "One of our target setters has been hit by the machine." I immediately headed to the area fully expecting to notify 911 in the next few minutes. When I arrived at the field the Line Ref and young man were sitting on the bench behind the sidewalk. The victim had a tiny cut above his left eyebrow, but his lower lip was swollen three times its normal size. I asked what had happened and he informed me this was the third time he'd been struck by the machine, twice nicking him in the lip, and once over the brow. Antiseptic and band aids were applied, and he was good to go, but refused to go back into the trap house with the demon machine.

- Another Midwinter tournament in Las Vegas, likely 1996 or 1997. Thursday started off with wind and sleet, and as usual, trap help proved to be vastly ill-prepared for such weather. We completed the first event and a rumor was spreading that the trap crews were preparing to strike. Sure enough, all the help ended up on the enclosed front porch of the clubhouse and announced they were done for the day. Over 500 shooters were waiting for the afternoon handicap and this situation would soon bring the tournament to its knees. I held a quick meeting with my wife, Lidia, and advised her to head to the bank as soon as possible and bring back $700 in ten- dollar bills. Meanwhile I gathered up dozens of small plastic ponchos I had purchased in the event of an emergency. When Lidia returned, I went out on the porch and addressed the group. I mentioned many competitors had come from far away to compete in the tournament and were counting on them. I needed to find out how many were willing to stick it out and would offer each of them a crisp $10 bill and a poncho if needed, but those interested were required to move to the field out front immediately. It was an amazing response. I stood in the doorway and handed out bill after bill as the help passed, some also accepting the ponchos. They were extremely appreciative. Finally, only one remained, and 70 were out on the field. The one remaining striker was invited off the property and the last I saw of him was walking out the front gate. A fifteen-minute call was issued over the PA for the handicap event and the tournament moved forward without further incident.

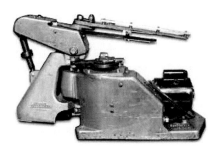

TO THE FAR NORTH

My hiatus from competitive trapshooting, at least in the lower 48 states, occurred when offered a position as shotgun operations manager of Alaska's Izaak Walton Recreation & Shooting Park (now Birchwood Recreation & Shooting Park) in the spring of 1982. This facility is located about 15 miles east of Anchorage. I had previously attended the Alaska State Trapshooting Championships at this location every year beginning in 1978. This was a direct result of meeting Claude McDowell and many of the Alaskan shooters making up a large contingency that attended Bob Taylor's 1978 "100 Grand" tournament the previous January. I often made a second trip to Alaska in September to take advantage of the fishing. I thoroughly enjoyed the country and the people.

After meeting with their Board of Trustees in March and working out the details, I accepted the position and started my new venture May 1, 1982. I was eager to learn more about the trapshooting and recreational shooting world from the other side of the counter, using my head instead of my trigger finger.

I thoroughly enjoyed my time up north and made just a few trips "outside" to participate in major trapshooting tournaments being held at that time. Flying became a new passion during this period, plus I found flying necessary to venture into areas off the beaten path. Obtaining a pilot's license and becoming a small aircraft owner provided me with opportunities seldom found in the lower 48 states.

When I first arrived at Izaak Walton, it was imperative to initiate a new program that had the potential to grow and provide steady return business. The club had been losing about $10,000 every winter when the colder weather and longer nights were prevalent.

During my final meeting with their Board in March, I had agreed to take the position totally on an incentive pay structure if they agreed to provide me with a minimum of six fully lit fields by September 1st. The seven Board Members glanced at each other as if bewildered. I finally spoke up and explained the need for the lighting. I would create evening Fall, Winter, Spring and Summer clay target leagues. It seemed apparent to me that this would be well received by the locals, even during the long winter months. Fortunately, the facility was within easy driving distance of a major population area of over 250,000, and a thriving economy. After more discussion, they finally agreed to meet the demand and the deal was done.

I had been on the job about a month when I met Jim Farley.

Jim was a supervisor with a company by the name of Magcobar Industries. Magcobar was one of the many oil field service companies in Alaska at that time. The entire Anchorage area was booming in 1982, largely due to construction and oilfield activity at Prudhoe Bay.

I casually mentioned to Jim that I wanted to start an evening trap & skeet league the first week of September. Teams would consist of five shooters; individuals would have a target spot based on their ability. One team vs another team each night with the ability for a team to win up to five points. Each team member would shoot 25 skeet and 25 16- yard trap each night for twelve weeks. I asked Jim if he knew anyone that would be interested in such a league. He thought about it for a minute or two and then said Magcobar alone could probably enter 8 teams. Oilfield personnel typically worked schedules of one week on, one week off, or two weeks on and one week off. Due to this shift work, our future league team rosters might have a dozen different names on it. At that point, I realized I was on the right track and evening league programs would be very successful.

I wasn't familiar with any established clay target league structures at the time, but I was very familiar with bowling leagues. As a sophomore and junior in high school, I had worked afternoons at a local bowling alley.

This led to a considerable amount of bowling. I once bowled in 52 consecutive jackpots on a Saturday. I also joined three different evening leagues. Two of these were handicap leagues. I became quite familiar with the handicap structure of these leagues and applied it to the new clay target leagues in Alaska.

Our first Fall Trap & Skeet League at Izaak Walton in 1982 consisted of sixteen 5-person teams. Many of the participants went on to enter the Winter league and we never looked back. The leagues quickly grew too large for just Wednesday and eventually Thursday evening was added. League night always offered a steak dinner, salad, and baked potato for five bucks. The food was kept simple, affordable, and consistent. This was also key to the league's growth. Several companies that participated brought in a blank check every afternoon. All team member's practice, ammunition, league entries, and dinners were covered by the check at the end of the evening. These check totals often exceeded $300. As far as I know, the fundamentals of these original leagues still continue at the Birchwood facility today.

Another thing I was able to implement while at Izaak Walton was the introduction of an Exclusive Park Membership, or EPM. This allowed qualified individuals to use the facility 7 days/week along with an account and self-invoicing. A security gate was installed, and pass-card holders were allowed entry on days the facility was closed to public shooting. It was at about this same time that I assumed the title of General Manager.

The combination of league activity and 7-day access are the two most important things I would highly recommend to any struggling clay target facilities out there today. Both will certainly contribute to a positive financial result.

Being in the far north posed problems similar to any other club in the colder climates. Like most trap facilities of that era, we used the Western handset trap machines. Automatic traps were still scarce. When the opportunity presented itself, we purchased two Remington 4100 automatic traps. This machine had an extremely short throwing arm and the target presentation was fair. It also had a very low capacity of 150 targets requiring it to be loaded following each full squad.

During the cold winter months of the Wednesday night league, I would send one of my staff out at least an hour early to turn on the skeet machines and the two automatic traps. When the 4100 is first turned on in the extreme cold, it will not rotate the throwing arm into battery. No matter how many times I cautioned staff about this, they would occasionally forget and pull the throwing arm into battery manually. This completely disrupted the timing of the machine. I can remember lying in the snow and ice on the outside of the trap house with temperatures in the teens and lower. To reset the timing, an inspection plate had to be removed from the front of the machine, and two large gear wheels re-meshed to the proper timing marks. I'm sure I wasn't the only 4100 user that had to do this.

Being on the coast, Anchorage doesn't experience weeks of extremely low temperatures such as the interior of Alaska. However, a very cold day or two may still occur every winter.

On one extremely, brutally cold Wednesday in January of 1984, the temperature plummeted to -28F. It finally warmed up to about -15 by 4pm. As usual, I sent someone out to turn on the skeet machines and the two Remington traps. I assisted and started with the machine in the high house of the skeet field directly in front of the clubhouse. I ran up the stairs, flipped on the switch, and headed back down the stairs. I heard the machine laboring and before I could get back up to turn it off, it had burned up the motor. The oil had almost solidified due to the extreme cold. Now I had to do a machine replacement in frigid conditions. Before any other machines were turned on, I sent one of my crew to the town of Eagle River to purchase a couple dozen cans of Sterno. When they returned, we placed these under all the machine oil reservoirs and lit them. About 30 minutes later we were able to turn on all the equipment and proceeded to start league on time. Amazingly enough, all 80 shooters showed up to shoot on the coldest Alaska night I experienced during my time there.

It wasn't long after that extremely cold night that I had the bright idea to equip each of the skeet fields with a diesel-fueled salamander heater. Some may know these as smudge pots. They're commonly seen around orchards and cold-climate construction sites. For those unfamiliar, they hold several gallons of diesel fuel in the bottom and have a fluted stack about 6' high. Once lit, in about 15 minutes they put out an extreme amount of heat.

Our Wednesday night league was 25 skeet and 25 16 yd trap. A full squad shooting a round of skeet takes a minimum of 25-30 minutes. If it was extremely cold, they could complete their skeet rounds in about 20 minutes, almost running from station to station. Having a place to warm up during the round on a cold winter night made a lot of sense to me.

The first night the heaters were provided, skeet rounds took 45 minutes to an hour to complete. I hadn't anticipated this. Everyone would shoot a station or two then gather around the heater. The following week all the heaters had disappeared.

For all the discomforts endured during Alaskan winters; the return of spring, summer and fall made it all worthwhile. Many days after closing the facility, I would jump in the plane parked right next door at Birchwood Airport. Within five minutes I could be looking down at Dall Sheep in the Chugach range or Black Bears on the other side of Knik Arm. If I felt like flying another 30 minutes or so, I could land on a beach and be fishing in a stream full of Pacific salmon. We had five varieties that returned to their freshwater birthplace to spawn depending on the time of year. Sockeye and Chinook showed up in late May and June, followed by Chum and Coho in August and September. The smaller Pink salmon arrived during the summer months every other year. While these are their formal names, the locals refer to them as "Reds, Kings, Dogs, Silvers and Humpies" respectively. Chinooks, or Kings, drew more fisherman from the lower 48 states due to their sheer size (Alaska rod & reel record 97 pounds, 4 ounces, from the Kenai River). I personally enjoyed the Silvers the most and have caught them up to 20 pounds at Silver Salmon Creek in late September.

Anchorage was the hub of ATA shooting in Alaska. Registered tournaments were held most months of the year, usually with attendance from Kenai, Soldotna, Palmer, Wasilla and the surrounding area. Occasionally we might have someone show up from Kodiak, Ketchikan, Seward or Homer. We established an annual 1000 target "Ironman" doubles event and the ATA Alaska State Shoot was held at our facility every year.

We hosted the last consolidated ATA Western Zone Tournament at Izaak Walton in July1986. This was combined with the ATA Alaska State Trap Championships. This may have been one of the most enjoyable tournaments I've ever been a part of.

We expected half of the attendance to be from out-of-state and wanted to put on a good show for everyone.

One of the events we planned during the week was a big outdoor BBQ at the club, featuring exclusively Alaska fish and game on the menu. I called on many of our local trapshooting hunters and fisherman for provisions, and boy, did they produce. We had pledges for halibut, salmon, moose, caribou, & black bear. We would also have cold draft beer on tap for the occasion. Now I just had to find someone to prepare and cook.

One of our members had provided me with a phone number for a gentleman known only as Ivory Joe. He operated a mobile BBQ unit and prepared food for different events in the Anchorage area. I called him up and told him what I needed. A couple of days later he showed up at the club to look the place over. He arrived on his Harley and looked exactly like an aging Hell's Angel with his beard and bandana. I showed him where we wanted to set up and where we intended to place his mobile cooking unit at the edge of a big top tent structure. I mentioned we would have a lot of out of town guests and wanted to have a very festive event. He looked everything over and nodded. The area selected faced towards Knik Arm and the Alaska Range in the distance. On a clear day, Denali was there in all its majesty though over 120 miles away.

At this point he tells me he has another friend that has a cooking unit very similar to his own and would like to have him come and work with him. I said great, sounds perfect. What is this going to set us back? He thinks about it for a few seconds, then smiled and said-"How about a hundred bucks and all the beer we can drink?" I confirmed we had a deal and shook on it.

Ivory Joe and his buddy showed up the day before the shoot started to set up their areas early. They each rolled in with two of the most impressive portable BBQ units I had ever seen. These were tandem-axle trailer mounted units, all chrome plated. The trailers were equipped with fancy custom wheels. Ivory Joe's buddy was a duplicate of him, only blond. Both were outstanding personalities and masters on their grills.

On the day of the cook-out, it was 75 degrees, sunny and calm. As perfect an Alaska day as you could ever hope for. As the program events of the day wrapped up, everyone started moving over to the party area. The shooters had been treated to the smell of good cooking all afternoon and were anxious to see what they were having.

It couldn't have come off more perfectly. All food was prepared to perfection and the guests were delighted. Plus, Ivory Joe and his buddy were the stars of the show. Their interaction with our guests was priceless and made for a truly unforgettable day. The only thing, I think we would have been ahead to have paid them additional cash rather than unlimited beer!

The second outstanding extracurricular event of the week was the party held at Tom Sokol's house on Big Lake. All of our out-of-town guests were invited. Tom cooked steaks on the grill, and Kodiak's Lou & Pat Schneider brought a large Igloo cooler filled with the largest King Crab legs I have ever seen. Most of the activity was on the large wooden deck that faced the lake during another picture-perfect afternoon and evening.

It was during this tournament that I broke the first 100 straight from the 27-yard line ever recorded in Alaska. (with 2 ¾ 8s which I used for all events) I believe this may have been the only 100 broken from any yardage at that time. I'm not sure if that still holds true today or not. Obviously, it was a perfect day providing perfect conditions.

There were so many other good people that supported my efforts at the Izaak Walton facility that I just have to mention a few of them; Jerry & Donna Urling, Jacob Allmaras, the McDowell family, Frank Woodfill, Maurice Oswald, the Sandland family, Dave Kaiser, Jacob Allmaras, Gerald Atol, Kelly McDaniel, Dave Thompson, Sam Weatherford, Eric Johnson, Don Hanks, Roger & Kathy Jones, Lou & Pat Schneider, the Jensen family, Rick Parmenter, Dave Diamond, and Ron Mimm. Ron and his construction crew added the room addition to the east side of clubhouse in 1985 for the cost of material.

The final year we were there, Lidia ran the kitchen with the help of lifelong friend, Paula Harbour. Paula provided all the great home-made pies before and during the 1987 Alaska State Trapshooting Tournament.

I've left many names out but a big thank you to everyone that made my time in Alaska so enjoyable and memorable.

TRANSITION

It was after I had finished my club management time at Izaak Walton and relocated to the Midwest in the fall of 1987 that I began to see a new, and surprising trend occurring at many trapshooting tournaments. It was quite noticeable that if conditions were less than ideal, many of those attending registered tournaments were not even participating. This was alarming and something I didn't understand at all, at least not at first.

During a late 1980's Tucson spring tournament, I witnessed an encounter that summed up the last two sentences in my previous paragraph. The day kicked off with a 16-yard event. Strong winds prevailed at Tucson that morning. In the sanctuary of the clubhouse dining and bar area were two tables of mostly well-known trapshooting All-Americans engaged in the game of Hearts.

Later the same morning, Dan Orlich entered the room, hair wind-blown and obviously just coming off the firing line. One of the card players acknowledged him and asked how it went. "94" Dan boomed, "And damned glad to have it!" Big Dan then asked- "How'd you guys do?" Anyone that knew Dan Orlich was well aware he didn't speak softly, especially in his later years. One of the card players finally looked up and stated "Uh, we didn't shoot this morning." Without hesitation, Dan immediately fired back "And you guys call yourselves All-Americans?" He left the area noticeably disappointed with what he had just heard. The room was crowded at the time with those having late breakfast or early lunch, and you could have heard a pin drop for several seconds following this exchange.

I'm uncertain of when, or where, this trend started, i.e., passing on events due to weather conditions. It's understandable that the elderly may elect to pass on an event under difficult conditions, but healthy, young and middle-age All-American Team Members? When you consider their actions are closely observed by hundreds, possibly thousands of shooters that admire and look up to them, the resulting impact can be confusing, and possibly quite negative.

I don't recall a single event during my competitive years that my squad mates or I dropped out of, or avoided, shooting an event due to inclement weather. Anyone that participated in Mid-Winter tournaments in Las Vegas, or the Golden West Grand in Reno, expected an array of weather that could range from very pleasant to downright horrible. Weather patterns during these events often contained high winds, sleet, rain, and possibly even snow. When packing for these tournaments, your suitcase consisted of the majority of the clothing you owned, including long underwear, wool sweaters and heavy windbreakers.

However, there were strong incentives to compete. There was always something of value to shoot for, be it cash, gold coins, silver, guns, or even automobiles. Plus, bad weather tended to narrow the field considerably. Many talented shooters were mentally defeated long before they took the firing line. I never quite understood this. A win was a win, regardless if the score was 89 or 99, plus options and purses provided better returns during events held under subpar conditions. I've always considered adverse weather and the wind to be an ally.

So, what created this new downturn in participation during less-than-perfect conditions? It appeared to be a combination of at least three factors; shooters were becoming more average conscious, competitive shooters were getting older, and there was a lack of substantial return.

Several things happened in the 1980s that led to two of these factors.

First- It appeared many gun clubs were easing up on target settings, with club operators realizing that shooters tended to return to facilities where they posted good scores. Less speed on the target combined with less angle, and scores improved. While arguably a good short-term business practice for the hosting club, what was this doing to the trapshooting game overall? This became even more prevalent in the 1990s as clubs advertised "premium" or "blueprint" targets at their facilities. It appeared there were also an increasing number of officials involved in target settings in an effort to increase their own proficiency. I believe it is fair to say the ATA average book is loaded with 27-yard shooters that have no business being there based on performance. Many will argue that after spending thousands of dollars and investing years of time, they earned their way there and deserve to stay if they so choose. The 27-yard pin is their badge of honor and a great accomplishment among registered shooters. I'm certainly not going to be an advocate against them. However, I'm confident in stating this group feels much better about turning in a 92 on what's commonly now referred to as "soft" targets rather than an 82 on targets as set in previous years. So, apparently this has become the new trend. Pandora's Box had been opened and there's no turning back. As a result, with higher scores commonplace, payouts on 25s and 50s dwindled, and increased high scores on the total divided up the purse to the point many stopped even entering options and purses. Oversight on the part of officials appeared to have vanished, somewhat due to the simple fact that many were over handicapped and enjoying the higher scores themselves. When you combine these target settings with a group of predominant 27-yard shooters that will never increase in yardage, the days of big money tournaments are over.

Second- Removal of the already dwindling money that's left in the game. Money is the root of all bad things that happen at ATA events. This may sound extreme, but this statement was made by a member of the ATA Executive Committee. During the Golden West Grand at Sage Hill in 2003, the Central Handicap Committee Chairman overheard one of our ATA Executive Committee members making this very remark. Later the same day, I approached this E.C. member and another ATA Official in the clubhouse and broached this subject. I told him that if he really believed this, why not take all the money out of the Grand American during his upcoming year as President of the ATA and test his theory. This led to considerable back pedaling, as it should have. When one considers that Grand American attendance historically doubled the day of the Preliminary Handicap, traditionally on Thursday. This huge influx of participants was due to those interested in one thing; a chance to win a few dollars to offset the considerable costs associated with their hobby.

There were a few sponsors during the 1980s/1990s period, often contributing additional trophies, life memberships, and similar prizes to tournaments they felt worthy. One of these went on to become a major sponsor of the "blueprint" target, popular at a West Texas club at that time. The same sponsor was also totally against compulsory purses in any ATA events and clearly stated he would not attend or support any tournaments that offered them. The clout of this sponsor was strong enough the Golden West Grand eventually discontinued compulsory purses in the final two handicaps of their program. These purses had been tradition for decades and a part of the most successful trapshooting tournament west of the Mississippi River.

I lost the support of this very sponsor while operating the Las Vegas Gun Club for a totally different reason than compulsory purses.

His spokesman (and driver at the time) came to me following one of our annual fall tournaments and said they wouldn't be returning, but rather putting their support behind facilities with a reputation of throwing "good" targets. His reference to "good" targets in this context referred to targets being thrown less than 48 yards for 16 yard & handicap, and no more than 40 yards in doubles. These were typical target settings of the spokesman's home club, well-known for high doubles scores and averages. We discussed target settings in Las Vegas as I was firm on 50-yard targets for 16 yard & handicap, and doubles targets set to a speed of 39-40 mph on the right-hand target when checked with an adequate radar gun. A direct quote from this spokesman followed that left me dumbfounded: "But Steve, what difference does it really make how far you throw doubles targets anyway?" Obviously, the ATA rulebook meant absolutely nothing to this gentleman. I said adios, and something like "don't let the door hit you on the way out".

To this day, I'm not sure if the actual sponsor knew of this conversation or not as I never brought it up to him. If he allowed his spokesman to represent him, then so be it, I wasn't going to compromise the integrity of the ATA rule book and Las Vegas tournaments in return for what was being asked.

Moving forward, I'm uncertain what will be the driving force behind registered tournament participation. It's certainly not for the opportunity to win a substantial amount of cash or even a coveted prize. Emphasis these days centers more around social interaction, comfort and convenience. Fortunately, there's a lot of youngsters that have entered the fray, and a good number of seniors. It's the lack of a group in between that creates concern. As the seniors eventually drop out there could certainly be a huge void that remains.

I'm sure there will be many successful state championship tournaments in the future, plus the numerous satellite grands. However, the days of private clubs and individuals hosting large events have come to a screeching halt, at least in the Western States.

I'll revisit this subject again in a later chapter.

PART 2

THE 1990S &
BEYOND

MORE RECENT TIMES

FAA vs LVGC

After leaving Alaska in 1987, I considered returning to the far North, but didn't want to repeat being subject to the boom & bust economy. To hedge this, I considered a position with the Federal Aviation Administration (FAA). I was already too old for control tower operations so decided to pursue a position in the Alaska region as a Flight Service Station operator dealing with general aviation. I was a pilot myself and this was a position I could relate to assisting other pilots.

This would require months of training prior to a four-hour written exam. I picked up training aids and workbooks at the Federal Building in downtown Kansas City in the summer of 1988.

While attending various tournaments that fall, and winter chain tournaments in January & February of 1989, I would return to the RV between events and study at every opportunity. I made plans to take the exam at the Federal Building in downtown Denver the end of February, following the Las Vegas midwinter tournament.

Meanwhile, I had been approached several times by Irv Goldstein, current operator of the Las Vegas Gun Club, formerly the Mint. I had attended the fall tournaments at this facility in 1987 & 1988, plus the midwinter event in 1989. During the last two of these tournaments, Irv had approached me and mentioned I should consider buying out the remaining portion of his lease and take over the facility.

Irv was a pawnshop owner in Tucson and was making trips to Las Vegas for the major tournaments. This extracurricular activity was apparently creating strife in the family and strain on his primary business. He had acquired the lease on the vacated 78-acre gun club property in the summer of 1986 from the State of Nevada Division of Parks. While I had some interest and recognized the potential, Irv wanted considerably more than I was willing to pay for the remaining 18 years of a 20-year lease.

The word of Irv and I having these discussions was apparently overheard and discussed in other circles. One day during the 1989 Las Vegas Midwinter tournament, I was sitting on a bench in front of the clubhouse between events. A gentleman came along and sat down beside me and introduced himself as Dwain Bell. He mentioned that he enjoyed coming to Las Vegas for tournaments and would like to see someone such as myself take over the facility and do something with it. He also mentioned he could provide financial assistance if needed. He left me his business card with his personal number and told me to call anytime. I didn't think too much about this at the time and stuck the card away in my billfold.

I finished the tournament, then travelled to Denver as planned. We found a KOA, parked the RV and unhooked the tow car. Lidia, now four months pregnant with our daughter, rode with me to find the location of the Federal Building that evening. I spent the next day with last minute cramming in preparation for the test.

The morning of the test, I arrived early at the Federal Building to discover a line of about 200 individuals outside waiting for the doors to open. Once opened, we streamed into a large area that consisted of four different classrooms with the partitions separating them removed. We were advised to be seated but not touch the thick test document that was face down on the desk. It was about 7:50 am, the test was to start promptly at 8am. About a dozen individuals served as floor monitors during the test. Their lead person stood at the head of the room with instructions on filling out the cover page accurately, and what to do once the test was completed. There would be a ten-minute break following the first two hours.

Finally, it was ready, set & go. Simultaneously, 200 of us turned the test document face up and began filling out required personal information on the cover page. A few minutes later, you could hear the pages being turned, and turned some more, and more. I realized that many of those in the room were looking for anything they could identify and answer properly, riffling through page after page. Within 30 minutes, over 3/4 of those in attendance had vacated, realizing they had absolutely no idea what they were doing taking this test.

As I proceeded through the pages, I was thankful I had dedicated so much time to studying. A huge proportion of the questions dealt with spatial relationships and sequencing. Had I not learned some of the tricks offered in the workbooks I would have certainly failed the exam miserably.

I finished about 30 minutes early, turned in the exam and left. When I returned to our campsite, we hooked up the car and headed east for the long trip to Bill Jacobsen's Silver Dollar Club in Florida. We would arrive in time to shoot at St. Petersburg and Sarasota prior to the Southern Grand.

Once we arrived at Silver Dollar, we were provided with an excellent RV space with plenty of room and shade trees. This would be our home for almost six weeks as we had decided we would stay through the Florida State Shoot.

Larry and Connie Bumsted were parked across the lane from us, and Phil and Marilyn Saia, were right next door. We spent a lot of time together and often made the trip to Paul's down at the Sponge Docks for a great seafood dinner.

I had purchased a mobile phone for the RV. Unlike cell phones of today, this was a large cumbersome unit that was in a vinyl bag and plugged into the dashboard cigarette lighter. It came with an antenna that stretched the cord from the unit, out the window, and to the top of the RV. Somewhat unsightly, but it worked.

Around the first week of April, I received a call from my parents that a letter had arrived from the Federal Aviation Administration. My mail was being forwarded to them while we were on the road. I asked my mother to go ahead and open it. She did so, then read that I had received a test score of 94.2, plus my five-point veteran's allocation resulted in 99.2. That was about it. The letter also mentioned if you scored less than 90 you would likely not be contacted in the future. It seemed at this point our future was heading in a new direction and Alaska may once again be in the picture.

We continued travelling all spring and summer hitting as many major events as possible. Towards the end of June, we were at the Salt Lake Gun Club for the Utah State Trap Championships. Our daughter's birth was due the end of July and we had decided she would be born in Alaska. My mother-in-law, father-in-law, and one sister-in-law still lived in Anchorage. Lidia took a flight from Salt Lake to Anchorage just in time to make the required 30-day minimum time allowed to fly before delivery.

I finished at Salt Lake, then went on to Laramie, Wyoming. Following their state shoot I drove the motor home to Kansas City, then boarded a flight to Anchorage.

When I arrived in Alaska, we were still a couple of weeks out before the big event. My father-in-law, Ron Rettig, mentioned the silver salmon were in and suggested he and I immediately go fishing for a couple of days. He kept a 44' Uniflite docked in the harbor at Seward.

It's an absolute miracle I survived this trip. I had never driven anywhere with him before and this proved to be a gut-wrenching two-hour drive down the 2-lane Seward Highway.

Along the way Ron was pointing out Dall Sheep on the mountainsides, slamming on the brakes, weaving and neglecting to keep an eye on traffic ahead. Many horn-blasts and flashing lights later we arrived at our destination.

We picked up a few supplies, loaded the boat and headed out onto Resurrection Bay, truly one of the most beautiful settings on Earth. We fished a while and caught a couple of salmon. Towards evening we pulled into a protected cove and dropped anchor. I was already tired from the long flight to Alaska combined with the nerve-wracking trip down the highway. I was ready for a good night's rest.

I woke up in the middle of the night, startled, as the boat's engine was running. I jumped up out of the berth, threw on my pants and shoes and made it topside. There was Ron at the helm. I asked what was going on. He said he got up to take a leak and discovered our anchor had not held. Subsequently we had drifted out of the cove and were bobbing around out in the middle of the shipping lane in the dark. We returned to the cove, dropped anchor again and I made for certain it was on solid ground before I returned to bed. The next morning, we fished a few more hours, then decided to have a good meal in Seward before heading back to Anchorage. Ron mentioned he was tired which was music to my ears. This would allow him to sleep while I drove on the way back.

We had an outstanding pizza for a meal. After eating, Ron mentioned he was now wide awake after a couple of Cokes and ready to go. Back up the highway for another adventure, this time in the twilight. It was terrifying.

My father-in-law was a very accomplished man, having served as a member of the Alaska House of Representatives and Senate in the 1960s and 70s. He also served as Alaska's Commissioner of Revenue and President of Alaska Mutual Savings Bank until his retirement in 1979. However, the thought of him making this trip back and forth from Anchorage to Seward on a regular basis was truly frightening.

Sometime later, I learned that Ron and my mother-in-law, Flor, were driving the return portion from Seward one evening, and **both** fell asleep. They awakened to a screeching sound and sparks flying off the guard rail raking the passenger side of the big Mercury Colony Park wagon. The guard railed saved them from plunging far below to an almost certain death.

I never rode as a passenger with Ron again, and forbid my wife and kids the same.

Shortly after my daughter's birth on July 25th, 1989, I flew back to Kansas City, loaded up the RV and drove to the Iowa State Shoot, then on to Vandalia for the Grand. Lidia and our brand-new baby girl flew to Vandalia as soon as the doctor allowed. Some of the shooter's wives hosted a fabulous baby shower at the beer tent!

We completed the Grand and travelled back to Kansas City for a few days to visit with the other set of new grandparents.

The following month I was back in Las Vegas for the fall 1989 tournament. Once again, Irv Goldstein approached me, but I felt the deal was not possible.

The Missouri Fall Handicap was a couple of weeks later and would wrap up our tournament schedule for a couple of months. We decided we would spend November and December with my parents and catch up on some lost time.

In early December, I received an unexpected telephone call one evening from Irv Goldstein. He had decided to drop his previous asking price to half of the original amount. This piqued my interest as I felt this was now possible as a successful business opportunity. After my call from Irv, I called Dwain Bell in California. He was excited about the possibility of moving this along. I asked if he could meet me in Las Vegas in three or four days and he said by all means. I called Irv back and set up the meeting. I would need to carefully review the lease and have a complete inventory of what I would be receiving.

Following the return call to Irv, I contacted a local travel agency and booked the flight to Las Vegas.

The next day, I drove to the travel agency to pick up the ticket for my flight. When I returned, the mail had delivered another letter from the Federal Aviation Administration. It informed me I had been selected to report to the Kansas City office of the F.A.A. for personal interview and mental evaluation. Following that, attend sixteen weeks of training in Oklahoma City in January, then expect to travel to Region 5 (Alaska) for Flight Service Station assignment. The timing of this was unbelievable.

That evening, I sat at the dining room table with my wife, my 4-month old daughter, and parents to discuss the future. On one

161

hand, I had lifetime security with an exclusive and highly respected branch of the Federal Government, on the other hand, I had who-knows-what as a gun club operator in Las Vegas. Realizing this may well be the most important decision of my lifetime, we considered all the pros and cons of both opportunities while having dinner that evening. It soon became obvious that my parents were leaning towards Las Vegas. They felt my background had prepared me for my own business in this field, plus, with the new grandchild, we would be considerably closer in Las Vegas than in Alaska. My father was also dealing with stage 4 prostate cancer at the time. Another potential pitfall with Alaska would be the actual location of the Flight Service Station. Many of these were in remote locations, far removed from city comforts, conveniences, and medical service. Living conditions could be quite spartan. There were certainly a number of important considerations, especially when an infant was involved. I decided to hold off responding to the F.A.A. until I returned from my trip to Nevada.

I arrived in Las Vegas a couple of days later and checked into the Holiday Hotel on the Strip. It was Wednesday and the gun club was supposed to be open that evening. I drove out later and found a make-shift sign indicating a back road to get in, avoiding the state park next door. One field was poorly lit directly in front of the clubhouse, but no one was shooting. I walked in to find Bill Mann inside behind the bar. I had known Bill for several years. A great guy, and a long-time employee of Harrah's in Reno; now in Las Vegas. Irv had hired him as a part-time manager of the gun club. Russ and Nancy Davenport were also there, and I believe Noel Humphrey. That was about it. I visited with Bill for a while, then returned to the hotel and made final preparations for my meeting with Irv and Dwain the next day.

When Irv and Dwain arrived, we decided to review the lease over lunch. Following this, we drove out to the gun club and determined what stayed and what was to go. It was a simple process and I decided I could make this work. Irv and I shook hands and went our separate ways. I would touch base with him within the next week to finalize everything.

Dwain and I then worked out the details of the financing. We visited an attorney's office to draw up documents, plus establish the new business as an S Corporation. I would borrow just enough to buy out the lease and cover operating costs & inventory to sustain the operation for six months; the rest was on me. It was either sink or swim at this point, we were all in.

Dwain returned to California and I returned to my hotel room feeling good about what had transpired and the direction I had chosen. I was about to fall asleep when the phone rang. It was an old friend and trap shooter from Missouri, Glen Torix. He just happened to be in town for the third fight between Sugar Ray Leonard and Roberto Duran the next evening. He had an extra ticket and invited me to attend the fight with him. This was held outside behind the new Mirage Hotel & Casino which had just opened weeks earlier. We were in the first row of elevated seats. Later, I discovered my ticket stub reflected an $800 purchase price.

I flew home the next day and shared the news of the trip. I contacted the Kansas City office of the FAA to let them know I would be declining the opportunity. The agent on the phone commented he had never seen a position declined so late in the process.

There was much to do in preparing for our departure. We would stay through Christmas, then start the move west.

I remember December 22 & 23 being extremely frigid in Kansas City that year with temperatures dipping to over twenty below zero which was rare to be that cold. The water filter on our RV froze solid and had to be replaced. We were very fortunate that was the only damage as our time left in Kansas City was rapidly coming to an end.

By Christmas Eve, temperatures had warmed considerably, and we spent a great Christmas with family and friends.

We had the motorhome, the tow car, and another car to move. On December 27th, I decided to drive our primary vehicle the almost 1400 miles to Las Vegas first, and parked it in one of the hotel parking garages. I then immediately flew back to Kansas City. If I remember correctly, after I arrived in Las Vegas, I parked the car in one of the hotel parking lots, took a cab to the airport and boarded the flight within two hours of my arrival.

On December 30th we packed up the motor home, hooked up the tow car and began our trip west, a little unsure of just what may be on the horizon. We spent New Year's Eve in a KOA just out of Albuquerque, NM. At midnight, we shared cold champagne while watching the festivities on TV.

We arrived in Las Vegas at about 3pm the next day; New Year's Day, 1990. We pulled into the Hacienda RV Park. This RV park grounds would later be developed and become the pyramid-shaped Luxor Hotel. The RV park would be our home for the next week or two while we looked for a place to live.

We settled on a new apartment complex located on the northwest side of town called Catalina Shores. This was conveniently located within just a few miles of the gun club.

After parking the RV at the club, we flew back to Kansas City once again to load up our furniture and belongings on a U-Haul truck. I would drive the truck out alone; another 1400-mile road trip. Once

I arrived Lidia and my daughter would fly back out and I could pick them up at the airport. It was a very busy time for us, but everything fell in place and the move was completed flawlessly.

Once comfortable in our new residence, all attention was directed towards licensing, fees, insurance, and corporate papers all being in their proper place. Plus, I was mailing programs and advertising the annual Mid-Winter Trapshooting Tournament to be held the end of February.

Everything came together; we opened on Valentine's Day.

We hosted our Mid-Winter Trapshooting Tournament the end of February with an attendance of about 300 competitors. I was pleased with the results but had encountered heavy rain at times during the competition and overall target count was down somewhat from projections.

It was important to establish a trap league on Wednesday evenings as soon as possible. Reliable and repetitive revenue would play a key role in our survival. By the middle of March, we accomplished this and had 12 teams composed of 60 shooters. Due to such poor existing lighting on the fields, I was leasing portable lighting on stands every week, plus I had built light bars to place immediately in front of the trap houses. It was crude but sufficient until we installed new and permanent field lighting. The Wednesday night trap league eventually grew to huge proportions and was largely responsible for the eventual financial success of L.V.G.C. Inc., dba, Las Vegas Gun Club.

I hired a bookkeeper and local accounting firm to accurately track our finances and prepare necessary reports for my landlord, The State of Nevada, Division of Parks.

The first year of operations ended with a loss of about $46,000. The second year a loss of $28,000. Waking up at 2am was common. There were more sleepless nights, 80-hour weeks, and second-guessing in these first two years than one could ever imagine. The third year we were in the black by $96. We had finally made it over the hump.

Lidia and I would share cold champagne once again.

Unfortunately, the miniscule profit in 1992 didn't come without considerable sacrifice.

In late April of 1992, we had planned to host a new, major trapshooting tournament, the "Silver State Open", featuring $20,000 in custom silver bars and coins. This was a 5-day event expected to draw 250-300 shooters its first year. As with any new major tournament, considerable planning, unique program development and marketing went along with this; all at considerable cost. Extra truckloads of targets were ordered along with a considerable amount of ammunition. Field staffing was ramped up and training of tournament staff initiated. A break-even or small loss would be acceptable to get the program established and be able to grow in subsequent years.

As the tournament drew closer, I was aware there was potential for civil unrest in southern California. A verdict was expected at any time for the trial of four police officers charged with the beating of Rodney King. I was receiving calls from fellow shooters that were apprehensive about leaving their homes in that area.

Sure enough, the verdict came down on April 29, acquitting all four officers. The resulting aftermath was historical.

I wasn't aware of all the circumstances working against us until I received a phone call one evening that week from Kurt Sachau. "Steve, they're showing major rioting in Las Vegas on the national news." Sure enough, national news coverage showed rioting and several fires that had broken out in Las Vegas. What they didn't show was the very limited area of North Las Vegas that was being impacted. The irresponsible news coverage made it appear all of Las Vegas was on fire. Regardless, many of our anticipated attendees sat this one out. Kurt, like others, were simply afraid to come and risk being caught up in a bad situation.

The financial impact to the tournament and our business was devastating.

Once the dust had settled it was obvious that I was going to have to make major cuts to our overhead for the business to continue forward. It would require that personal expenses be trimmed down to a bare minimum.

For the previous year we had been leasing a home in the Painted Desert development and were approaching the end of the lease period. I sat down with Lidia one evening and shared the grim news regarding the current financial status of the business.

Our daughter would be 3 years old in a couple of months and our son was only 16 months.

We made the decision to give up the house to eliminate a considerable amount of pressure on the business account. Furnishings and many personal items would have to be temporarily stored. I would develop an area at the gun club to park our RV and we would use its 264 square feet as shelter until better times arrived.

I chose a level site with access to septic and ample shade on the west side. I installed water and electric lines, built a large redwood deck, and a 6' cedar fence that enclosed a small, but newly sodded yard. The RV was backed in, awning extended, and this would be home for the next 14 months. Fortunately, our RV was equipped with washer & dryer which helped considerably.

Thinking back, some of our best times may have been during this period. I can remember many evenings stepping out on the deck under the awning and watching new episodes of "Lonesome Dove" on TV. The State Park was just to our south and the large irrigation systems kicked on during the summer evenings. This created a cooling effect that benefited our location considerably.

At that time, there was a vendor in the park with a horse-drawn wagon that went back and forth on the park road during the day. He used to stop by our east entry gate to allow our daughter to get on the wagon and ride along with him. She was his best customer and I'm sure this was the beginning of her love affair with horses.

We were all in very close quarters, but the kids loved it and had run of the entire property when the business was closed.

Obviously, things improved dramatically over the next year.

Fourteen months later we purchased a ranch-style home in August of 1993, with an acre of property, thirty mature trees, and full lawns, front and back. At first the kids exhibited separation anxiety as their bedrooms were on the other side of the living room, opposite our master bedroom. The first couple of nights, they brought in pillows and blankets and slept on our bedroom floor.

There was a corral and tack room in the back. Before long there was a Welsh pony living in the corral that my daughter rode and trailered to shows for several years.

Lidia and I still reside at the same location today.

We would operate the Las Vegas Gun Club (previously the Flamingo, Sahara, Sahara-Mint, Mint, & Landmark) from February 1, 1990, until our final day on December 19, 2009. Our closing date was also the soft opening of the new sixty-four million-dollar Clark County Shooting Park, now known as the Clark County Shooting Complex.

TRIALS & TRIBULATIONS
OF A NEW BUSINESS

Within a few days of the 1990 New Year and our arrival in Las Vegas, I made the trip downtown to apply for the four business licenses we would need. As our 26-page lease stated we would operate under the County, the Clark County Government Center was my first stop.

I arrived at the Business License Department and filled out the applications. The clerk entered the information into her computer, then stopped and said- "This location is actually under the City of Las Vegas jurisdiction; not Clark County." I was surprised as this was different than stated in our lease. I assumed this was no big deal and proceeded to City Hall.

A few minutes later I arrived at the City of Las Vegas Business License Department, I was greeted by Eddie Raines, Acting Chief, License Division. I can remember him very clearly; likely due to the shock I was about to receive.

I requested the four different license applications- General, Retail Sales, Restaurant, and Bar. Eddie proceeded to bring me the different applications then mentioned; "By the way, the Bar License is $60,000 up front." I'm sure my jaw probably dropped a bit when hearing this.

City of Las Vegas bar licenses are limited, transferable, and expensive. After the initial $60,000, you're still required to pay $1500 quarterly to maintain. This was out of the question for us as the bar was strictly a sideline, not our main business. I discovered that the same "tavern" license issued by Clark County is $300 quarterly, period.

In general, every bar business north of Sahara Avenue is licensed by the City; everything south of Sahara is licensed by the County, which includes all the major strip resorts.

At the root of my problem was that the State Park next door to the gun club used to be a City Park. What had been Tule Springs Park, established in 1964 by the City of Las Vegas, became Floyd Lamb State Park in 1977. As we were attached to the adjacent property, the State of Nevada, Division of Parks was my landlord, but any necessary licensing was still attached to the city. I found this to be absurd, and attributable to someone too lazy to update records properly.

Having a bar at a gun club is a tricky business, and likely completely impossible these days as it would be considered extremely politically incorrect. However, this facility had operated for forty years prior to this under several names; probably due to the particular trap tournament host Hotel & Casino at the time. Examples- The Flamingo, the Sahara, the Sahara-Mint, the Mint (which had the longest duration), the Landmark, and finally, the Las Vegas Gun Club. For many years, shooters had come to this facility and had developed certain expectations of what a proper gun club in Las Vegas should provide.

The first year I attended a Las Vegas Midwinter Trap Tournament was in 1967. It was the Sahara Gun Club at the time. Entering the clubhouse for the first time was a total surprise. Rows and rows of slot machines, Blackjack tables, a crap table, roulette table and wheel of fortune. The cashier's area included drawers with chip racks allowing chip purchases for the gaming. The bar was packed with wives and girlfriends and those that had finished their shooting for the day. Buffets capable of handling hundreds of shooters and guests were set up providing excellent breakfast and lunch.

My intent in 1990 was to recapture a portion of that era and the bar would be the centerpiece. The hardwood backbar was truly an amazing piece of history; over 150 years old, having come from a long-gone establishment in northern Nevada. The backbar was 66 feet long and 11 feet high, adorned with back-lighted stained glass and mirrored shelves. It almost appeared that the building must have been constructed around it.

At some point in the future, I also wanted to pursue a Restricted Gaming License that would allow us up to 15 slot/video poker machines of which at least 8 would be installed in the bar top. These would provide our customers with extra Las Vegas-style entertainment and, hopefully, provide the business with extra revenue. If everything went according to plan, we would end up with five diversified revenue streams that would contribute to the success of the business; and that all five would be critical for the business to remain solvent year-round-

- Trap admissions

- Pro Shop (including ammo, accessories and gun sales)

- Restaurant

- Bar

- Gaming

However, the bar/tavern license would need to be in place before the gaming license would be considered. This was the beginning of a quest that would take over four years to resolve.

In the meantime, I appeared before the Las Vegas City Council on many occasions to obtain a temporary event license to allow the bar to operate. The mayor of Las Vegas at that time was Jan Laverty Jones, and was always pleasant to go before. However, there was always a councilman or two that expressed reservations about the idea of guns and alcohol together which was totally understandable. Sooner or later, obtaining these special permits was going to become a problem. I finally tired of this and decided to tackle the problem head-on.

In July of 1991, I arranged a meeting with a representative from the State Attorney General's Office, Mark Gann, and an Administrator of Nevada's Division of Parks, Wayne Perock. Mr. Perock had written the gun club lease and his name, accompanied by signature, appeared at the bottom of the 26-page document.

I drove the 400-plus miles to meet them one afternoon in the lounge of the newly opened Little Mondeaux Gun Club at Genoa, NV. Neither were aware of the other attending, or what the meeting was about.

Wayne arrived first. We exchanged greetings and ordered beverage and snacks. A few minutes later Mark arrived. Both were surprised to see each other. They were casually acquainted with each other and worked in the same building in Carson City. After a bit of jovial interaction one of them finally asked what we were meeting about.

I said- "Gentlemen, we have a slight problem." I handed a copy of the lease to each of them. "I'm obligated to a 20-year lease that states I can operate the bar at the Las Vegas Gun Club under County licensing. When I went to the County for licensing applications, I found out that wasn't the case. Mr. Perock wrote, and signed, the lease."

Quite suddenly, the atmosphere changed, not quite as jubilant as before. It wasn't my intention to sound threatening, but I needed to drive the point home as the future of our business and my family's livelihood depended on it. I continued- "Does it seem realistic that should the State Division of Parks wish to run their own concession and acquire a bar license, they would be required to pay the City of Las Vegas $60,000? This seems to be a situation in which the prince would be taxing the king and just makes no sense to me."

Wayne was clearly embarrassed, and Mark finally broke the tension. "Look, let me take a look at this and see what I can do." Things lightened a bit. We had a conversation regarding how the facility had been doing up to this point, and the recreational shooting business in general. Shortly after, we parted ways.

Following the meeting, I was aware there would be other issues coming up that could present obstacles. Even if the licensing situation is resolved, we would still need permission from the State Division of Parks to allow gaming. Plus, if licensing should change over to Clark County's jurisdiction, we'll have to go before the Board of County Commissioners for approval of the bar operation. There were a considerable number of potential pitfalls.

Six months went by and I received a thick envelope in the mail from the Nevada State Attorney General's office. There were copies of many court cases enclosed that were similar to my situation, but nothing quite identical. Finally, at the end of all these cases was the

175

document I was looking for; a letter directly from the Nevada State Attorney General stating that, in his opinion, the Las Vegas Gun Club should not be licensed under the City of Las Vegas. This was a tremendous relief. Now I could proceed.

A few days later I returned to the City of Las Vegas Business License department and presented a copy of the State Attorney General's letter to Eddie Raines. He said he would present this to the City Attorney, which was Roy Woofter at that time.

I left, assuming it would be another six months before I received any news.

Just a few weeks later I received a letter from the City Attorney's office, stating the City of Las Vegas relinquished all licensing jurisdiction over the Las Vegas Gun Club. This was tremendous news. Slowly and surely, we were overcoming obstacles to reach our goal.

The following week, I returned to the Clark County Business License Department, armed with copies of my two letters. The clerk took these into an office occupied by Mahlon Edwards, Counsel for Clark County. He reviewed both letters, spent a few minutes on his computer, then came out to the counter to see me. He informed me that even with the City relinquishing licensing jurisdiction, Clark County couldn't accept us as we appeared nowhere in County documentation. We were off the grid as records had never been updated when Tule Springs City Park became Floyd Lamb State Park. Another hurdle.

After leaving the County building, I called my attorney, Fred Kennedy, to discuss the recent development. Fred was an active trap shooter and frequented the gun club. After a few minutes of dwelling on this he finally said – "You know what, you've done everything you could possibly do to correct this situation. If I were you, I would go ahead and pay the $250 Federal fee (ATF), and operate your bar. Who's going to shut you down? The City of Las Vegas relinquished jurisdiction, Clark County doesn't want you, and there is no State jurisdiction. There's no one to shut you down!" And, that's exactly what we did for the next 18 months. However, without Clark County licensing, I was dead in the water regarding the gaming license.

Fast forward to Summer1993. I'm standing in the pro shop one day and out of the blue a stranger walked into the clubhouse and introduced himself as Dave Etters. He was the slot route manager for CDF. He was also an acquaintance of Bill Mains, our primary trophy supplier, Mains Enterprises. I had shared some of the difficulties I had encountered the previous two years with Bill; he in turn, had expressed these to Dave Etters. Dave was also looking for new business partnerships.

Dave mentioned that he knew quite a few people with Clark County and with my permission he would pursue this. I said we would certainly appreciate anything he could do.

Another month or so went by and Dave returned. He mentioned that our requested County licensing applications would be sent to us within the next two weeks.

In the meantime, he wanted Lidia and I to each begin the process of applying for a Restricted Gaming License. These are very long and detailed applications, and, if everything is correct, final approval can take a year or longer. We started the process.

Sure enough, Clark County sent all requested license applications. Licensing for bar or gaming is considered a "privileged" license and must have approval from the 7-member Board of County

Commissioners. We completed all the applications and waited for our privileged licensing applications to appear as an agenda item at a future BCC meeting.

When the first meeting came around, it was just for the bar licensing only. We arrived at the chambers and waited for our item to come up. Finally, it was announced, and we were called up to the podium. One of the Commissioners read the Agenda Item and called for comments from the other board members. As expected, discussion immediately began to point out the negative connection between guns and alcohol. I began to believe our attempt could result in failure. When I was finally asked to speak, I commented on the popular history of our unique facility, and the bar was key to that. Future customers would be counting on reliving some of the past at our facility. Totally unexpectedly, long-time Commissioner, Paul Christensen, stated he was very familiar with our facility and had been there many times. Had never witnessed or heard of any issues due to trapshooting and a bar sharing the historic property. He mentioned that what I had said was true, and he made a motion for immediate approval of our license. The motion was accepted, and the vote was unanimous in favor by all 7 Commissioners.

To say we were relieved was a huge understatement. Had it not been for Commissioner Christensen's recommendation, our future could have turned out very differently.

The Restricted Gaming License application, along with all other related documents & supplements required, consisted of about 30 pages for each of us. It asks for detailed information such as-

- Employment records from 18 years of age

- Birth records

- Residence addresses for past 25 years

- Character references; minimum of 5

- Current and past financial disclosures

- Copies of all corporate papers

- All arrests, detentions, or litigations

And it goes on and on from there. This takes a considerable amount of time and research. After the Gaming Control Board eradicated mob activity in Nevada, they were determined to prevent it from ever gaining a foothold again.

After multiple reviews of our applications, we were finally satisfied and submitted them to Nevada Gaming Control.

Within a few days we were assigned to Dennis Lauderdale, one of the gaming control board's agents. He drove out to the gun club and introduced himself. He also asked what we had in mind for location. We told him at least 8 bar-top video poker machines, and possibly 6 free-standing models. He recommended a security camera surveillance system capable of covering and recording all gaming activity. We assured him this would be completed immediately.

About a month later, I received a phone call from Dennis. He asked if I was sure I had disclosed everything related to tickets, arrests, and so forth. I said I had. He paused a moment and then asked; "What about Paola, KS?" I wracked my brain a minute and thought "Paola, KS?" I asked if he could give me a hint regarding the date. "How about September 1967?" Now I recognized the date, and the incident, but had totally forgotten about it.

About a week into the dove hunting season in 1967, three of my high school friends asked if I would come with them to a great dove hunting location discovered about an hour south of Kansas City. They had gone on opening day and found lots of doves, but none of them could hit any birds. I said sure, I wasn't doing anything else, other than preparing to enter the military a month later.

The next day they picked me up and we headed south. I sat in the back seat and attempted to give verbal pointers on how to hit a flying dove. We drove about 45 minutes or so before leaving the paved road and drove another 30 minutes on a rural gravel road. Our driver finally pulled over as we'd reached our destination. We were out in the countryside now; there was a farmhouse another quarter mile or so up the road. While getting our guns out I noticed there were a lot of doves in the area. We walked about a half mile or so into the field and spread out.

After about 30 minutes of shooting activity, a police car pulled into the same area we had parked. And, he had his lights flashing. I told the guys we had better go down and see what's going on. As we approached, I noticed the vehicle was a Kansas State Highway Patrol car. That struck me as odd, being we were in Missouri. When we got closer, one of us asked if there was a problem. He then informed us we're all under arrest for trespassing! Our buddy that was driving said this must be a mistake as he was given permission to hunt this area a few days prior by the lady that lived in the farmhouse down the road. The officer said it was her husband that made the complaint.

The trooper then asked to see our hunting license. We all produced our Missouri hunting license. He then informed us that we're one quarter mile into Kansas, and under arrest. Another patrol car showed up and the two cars, one ahead & one behind, escorted us apparently dangerous felons to Paola, KS, the County seat. Mug shots were taken, we were all fingerprinted, and thrown into the slammer. None of us had enough money to post a bail. Fortunately, the judge chose to see our case that afternoon. We're all taken to the courthouse to face our accuser. It turned out the wife had to confess she had given permission that the husband was unaware of. The trespassing charge was dropped, but fines of $10 each were imposed for not having a Kansas hunting license. I had enough money with me to cover two of us, but one of my buddy's girlfriends had to drive the 50 miles down with money to pay the fines for the other two.

Some dove hunting trip! And this was on my record. After explaining, Agent Lauderdale laughed and said he could see how that could have been forgotten. He assured me it would not be an issue with our applications moving forward.

While waiting for news regarding our gaming application, I continued to move forward, submitting requests for limited gaming from both the Nevada Division of Parks, and Clark County. These would be contingent on both of our applications being approved by the State Gaming Control Board. This part turned out to be less difficult than I had originally anticipated. Division of Parks approved my request almost immediately, and we went before the BCC once again and were approved unanimously for the Restricted Gaming License; contingent on being approved by State Gaming Control. Our case was championed once again by Commissioner Christensen. Everything now just hinged on Gaming Control's approval of our applications. Any glitch with either one of the applications would result in both being tossed out.

Months went by and I finally received a call from Dennis Lauderdale. Our applications had been approved for content, but we were required to make a personal appearance before the Gaming Control Board for final approval. The date was set, and we would be seventh on the Agenda.

When the day rolled around, Lidia and I made the trip across town to stand in front of the board. We're excited and apprehensive at the same time. It had taken over four years to get to this point and it could all go away in an instant.

The six items on the Agenda ahead of us ranged from new license applications, re-submittals, and transferring locations. All six were flatly denied. It was our turn and there was certainly no momentum on our side. Bill Bible was Chairman of the Gaming Control Board at the time, but I knew nothing about him or how he might view our application.

So, there we are, standing in front of the board members, they in their elevated positions in front of us. Chairman Bible reviewed some of our paperwork then looked at me and asked- "This is the old Sahara-Mint Gun Club isn't it?" I confirmed that it was, and that we were trying to breathe some life back into it. After a few minutes he addressed the other board members and that he saw no reason this should not be approved. They all agreed. We're ecstatic. We thanked the board, and as we were leaving the room Dennis Lauderdale came up and congratulated us. This felt like a reward for everything you've done right in your life. I then asked Dennis- "I'm curious. What does one have to do to be considered for a full-blown resort gaming license?" He said- "Well, for one thing, we look at every check you have ever written, or received, in your lifetime."

I remember at the time thinking how unbelievable that seemed.

From beginning to end, the restricted gaming license process took over twelve months in all to finalize.

There was no doubt the investigating agent had done his homework. We heard from several old friends and neighbors that learned we were in Las Vegas as a result of the investigation. There's no doubt, the Nevada Gaming Control Board is extremely thorough.

In January of 1994, the CDF slot company installed 8 new video poker machines in the fully licensed bar of the Las Vegas Gun Club. (we would add two more over the following years)

This would be a welcome addition for the 45th Annual Midwinter Trapshooting Tournament coming up the following month. Mission accomplished. We could now move forward firing on all cylinders. No more sleepless nights; at least for another five years.

During our large tournaments I often took a quick break once I was assured all the trap help had showed up, and all the fields were full of squads. For me personally, most of the work was during the 6 months prior to the beginning of the tournament.

On more than one occasion, someone would sit down on the bench next to me and say- "You know Steve, I'm thinking about getting into the gun club business after I retire."

I just didn't have the heart, or the time, to explain what they may be getting themselves into.

LEAGUE NIGHT

For almost nineteen years, trap leagues were held on Wednesday evenings at the Las Vegas Gun Club.

To get it started, I sent out many cold calls by fax machine to target businesses in 1990. I used this process the first two years then quit to assure we weren't overwhelmed beyond our capacity.

Three large 4' x 8' custom scoreboards were mounted end-to-end on the wall behind the league secretary's counter. These boards could handle up to 64 league teams if necessary. They could also be flipped over as "Special Event" boards during major ATA events. Spring & Fall leagues spanned twelve to fourteen weeks each, and Summer & Winter leagues spanned ten to twelve weeks each. The only reason league night activity would be interrupted was due to a major week-long trap event or a holiday. I can only recall cancellations due to weather once or twice.

My son and daughter literally grew up in the clubhouse, both participated in leagues at an early age. During this period, over 500 different 5-person teams competed. Our largest league was 56 teams (280 shooters) in the Spring of 2006. Obviously, the Wednesday night trap league was the financial backbone of the facility.

One of our league shooters, Archie Jones, never missed a league night for the entire duration of the 19-year period. Archie was presented with a plaque after achieving participation in 50 consecutive leagues, never missing a night. He was proclaimed as "Mr. Wednesday Night Lights." Amazingly enough, Archie's string is still intact at the time of this writing. He is now well over 100 consecutive leagues, and still going strong.

Archie Jones- Mr. Wednesday Night Lights!

Besides the shooting activity, there was always good food available and social activity at the bar once shooting was completed. We initially provided eight bar-top video poker machines for added entertainment and supplementary income. We eventually added two additional machines. Royal Flushes and big winners were common and stimulated activity.

League shooting typically wrapped up between 9:00 and 9:30 pm, then we'd have a giant Annie Oakley or two. The One-Shot Pot was held for many years, along with the 50-50 raffle. The Nevada State Trapshooting Association (NSTA) sold tickets all evening for $1 each, raising hundreds of dollars for the association. Jim Talley served as NSTA President during this period and his wife, Marge, handled the weekly ticket sales.

My daughter, Fabriana, center, and her all girls team, "TLC", were a fixture of the Wednesday Night Trap League for many years

All the shooting activity was concluded by 10:00 pm which was our curfew to keep peace with the neighbors. In addition, the last seven or eight years of operation, we offered a Texas Hold'em tournament that started around 9:30 each evening. Typically, 30-40 entries, with a blind structure that assured the tournament would be over around midnight. We even established a points-race to determine annual Las Vegas Gun Club Hold'em Champions. Non-players socialized in the bar area, and many would gather around the wood stove on cold winter nights; flames could be seen glowing through the glass in the door.

I thoroughly enjoyed hosting the Wednesday Night Trap League. Literally thousands of league shooters participated in the evening festivities. It was "hump night" for most, and the perfect break to their work week.

I can vividly remember thinking on many of these evenings that these are "the good old days" we're experiencing right now, but no one realized it yet. There most certainly will come a time they will.

Team "Dirtbaggers" dominated the
Wednesday Night Trap League for 10 years

THE ACCIDENTAL $5000 WINNER

Wednesday night at the Las Vegas Gun Club was league night from March 1990, until the club closed in December 2009. Spring & Fall leagues typically consisted of 240-250 shooters; Summer & Winter averaged about half that number.

In the mid-90s we started selling raffle tickets for $1 each for the new "One-Shot Pot". At the end of each night we would draw one ticket out of the raffle drum and that shooter earned a shot at the money collected. The shot was quite difficult as the shooter had to stand on the 27-yard line of post 5 and shoot at a target that was released from one entire field to the left. Each week's winner was provided with a single 3-dram, 7 ½ Winchester silver bullet. Once the drawing winner's name was called over the PA, the entire clubhouse emptied out with onlookers and I carried the lone shell on a silver platter to the shooter, along with a shot of peppermint schnapps.

The lucky shooter was allowed to look at a maximum of two targets before calling for and shooting at the third. The progressive pot accumulated for months as nobody could break the target. As the money accumulated, ticket sales increased exponentially with the pot finally exceeding $5000 after a single year of existence.

Diane Kim was a Las Vegas native and a hostess at the Gold Coast Hotel & Casino. She and her daughter, Alana, participated in league for many years, and occasionally entered ATA events, but scores were rarely in ATA competitive range; 18-20 of 25 was about the norm. Diane's name was called as the drawing winner one night. I walked with her over to the shooting position, quickly explained the rules, and presented her with the lone shell. She loaded her Beretta auto, asked to see a target, then another. She took a deep breath, mounted the gun and called for the target. It was an extremely hard right angle and Diane didn't even move the gun as apparently, she hadn't even seen it. I finally hollered at her that it was getting away. She made a wild stab to the right and pulled the trigger. To everyone's absolute astonishment (including hers) the target broke into about 3 pieces. The entire facility went completely berserk with cheering and clapping. She was awarded the cash and celebrated her victory with everyone late into the night.

A picture of Diane, proudly displaying over $5,400 in $100 bills, hung on the wall at the end of the bar until the time of the club's closing.

DIANE KIM Diane Lea Kim, 61, of Las Vegas, passed away May 10, 2012. She was born Dec. 3, 1950, in Las Vegas, and was a lifelong resident of Nevada. Diane was a second-generation native Nevadan. She worked for Michael Gaughan for 30 years from cocktails, to dealing, to the pit and surveillance. When Diane was young, she rode dirt bikes, a Harley and could ride with the best of them. She was very athletic. Diane might say one big accomplishment was hitting the one-shot pot for $5,000 at the Las Vegas Gun Club. She was a skeet and trap shooter. Diane got her first gun at age seven, a 22 rifle with a scope. She was preceded in death by her father, Lt. Frank Kim, a 31-year veteran of Metro. Diane is survived by her mother, Charlotte Kim; and loving daughter, Alana Lea Kim, both of Las Vegas. Visitation will be from 11 a.m.-1 p.m. Thursday May

17, with services following, both at Davis Funeral Home, 6200 S. Eastern Ave. Burial following, at Davis Memorial Park.

Diane, may you rest in peace, knowing you provided all of us at the Las Vegas Gun Club with one of our most exciting nights ever and will be remembered by many for year to come.

KAY, RAY, AND THEIR FEATHERED FAN

At the conclusion of the Las Vegas Fall Trapshooting Tournament in 1991, Kay Ohye and Ray Stafford broke 99s to tie for the final handicap. Many shooters and guests stayed around to watch the shoot-off between these two accomplished and long-time All-American shooters.

The shoot-off field was just east of the clubhouse, directly in front of Wendall Schroll and Phil & Jan Lombardi's vendor spots. Everyone gathered round as the two took the firing line. After the ceremonial "Ready? Let's see one", Kay led off, broke his target, then on to Ray. Ray called with his usual "aaaaaahhhhhh" as he had done for many years.

Immediately following his shot, there was a loud "aaaaahhhhhh" heard from the crowd, as if mocking Ray. Everyone was looking around, including the shoot-off referee, but, thank goodness to proper ear protection, it was apparent this was not heard by either shooter. This took me totally by surprise as I couldn't imagine anyone doing such a thing. The sequence repeated itself, and once again the echoing "aaaaahhhhhh" was heard from the crowd. What the hell? The spectators were turning around and glaring at one another as they hadn't determined who the culprit was, but obviously among them. At this point I walked over to where the sound seemed to be coming from and discovered Phil Lombardi (also known as 3-fingers Louie) with a long pole in his hand trying to dislodge his pet Cockatoo from about 8' up in a tree. He finally succeeded and the mystery was solved.

Kay went on to win the shoot-off. I never determined if the shoot-off results had anything to do with the imposter or not.

EARL SCRIPTURE

Without a doubt, Earl Scripture may have been one of the most controversial and polarizing shooters of his time.

Earl was an outstanding talent and he, along with Dan Bonillas, Neal Crausbay, Gary Sherrod and yours truly, were members of our record-setting squad of 998 X 1000 at Vandalia in 1992. He had the gift of gab and an extraordinary personality. During events at the Grand American, it was not uncommon to arrive at the next trap to find it backed up and the gun rack full. Not a problem for Earl, he'd just stick his TM1 in the trash can, much to the amusement of onlookers.

Earl made several trips to support my events at the Las Vegas Gun Club and I always enjoyed having him there. His outgoing personality and willingness to spend time talking and socializing with anyone made him a crowd pleaser among the country's best shooters.

His shooting ability was never in doubt. He and Ross Warren once continued perfect for 10 rounds of overtime following 200-straight. This was after widening and lengthening the targets. They were finally deemed Singles Co-Champions at our 1993 Fall Tournament, allowing the planned evening activities and Special Event to proceed!

Earl was involved in the operation of at least three different gun clubs in the 80s and 90s. Rumor was that he was relieved of his position in Indiana after mounting the tail feathers of federally protected birds of prey on the clubhouse wall. I happened to be in the cashiering line at the Grand the year this happened. I was between two very vocal members of the club in question that were openly discussing this, so received my information first-hand.

He found a home for a while after taking on the manager's position at the El Paso Gun Club. He often hosted "Bullethons" allowing shooters to come in and register thousands of targets. He was a great host, and prepared excellent food for all, though target-settings conforming to existing ATA rules were questionable.

Additional stories began circulating about scores being turned in from the El Paso club that may have not actually been shot. There were even scores turned in for someone that had died the previous year.

About a month before our 1996 Fall Trapshooting Tournament, I received a call from a fellow named Forest Peterson. He asked if he could be a line referee for our tournament. He had worked at the El Paso club for quite some time and was experienced. He arrived in Las Vegas a couple of weeks later. During a conversation he explained he needed to leave El Paso as everything at the club there was about to blow up. I didn't ask him to explain.

The following year the ATA requested several months of registered shoot scoresheets and documents from Earl. He said he couldn't provide these as they were in the back of his Corvette which had just been recently stolen.

A well-known All-American shooter from the upper Midwest told me that he had driven his motorhome to El Paso before going on to

Arizona for several of the winter chain tournaments. He wanted to spend a couple of days warming up on the practice fields. One day he was shooting handicap by himself and ended up only missing one target out of the hundred. The scorekeeper said- "Hey, we'll register this one!" The shooter informed him it didn't work that way. The scorekeeper responded- "We do it all the time." I'm very confident this shooter was speaking the truth, and anyone that knows him would also believe this incident occurred.

Eventually, Earl was banned from the ATA for life. This was unfortunate as he had many friends and supporters in the ATA and was an outstanding shooting talent.

In my opinion, Earl was just born about 100 years too late. You couldn't help but like him, but it seemed he always had one toe just slightly over the line.

DICK MARASCOLA & DON CARLSON

Possibly one of the most unusual beginnings of an enduring friendship that I've ever had the privilege to witness first-hand.

In 1996 at the Las Vegas Gun Club (formerly the "Mint Gun Club") a shooter by the name of Don Carlson arrived from Liberty Hill, Texas. He had travelled out to compete in the Mid-Winter Tournament with his new Browning Recoil- less shotgun. I became aware of Don's presence when he sought me out to handle a situation for him on the first day of the event.

After introducing himself, we exchanged a few pleasantries, and I asked him what I could do to make his visit with us more enjoyable. He thought about it a minute, then cocked his head and said- "you need to fire that sonofabitch right over there" and pointed to Dick Marascola, our personnel in charge of the handicap table. This caught me off guard as Dick had been a fixture of major trapshooting events at our facility for many years while serving as Chairman of the Central Handicap Committee. I asked what on earth had happened and he said- "He's just a rude bastard and gave me a hard time when I signed up this morning". I told him I would check on this and try to enjoy his time shooting with us.

Later, when Dick was caught up on his duties and alone, I walked over to find out what grievous act had occurred. "Jesus Christ" he says, "this guy shows up in the middle of a long line of shooters with a handful of papers, hand-written scores and dates, scraps flying everywhere, and nothing updated on his handicap card regarding averages. I told him to get everything current on his card and then come back and present it to me so I can properly classify him. He didn't like that." I added something to the fact he was probably a new shooter and unfamiliar with the responsibility of the shooters when entering ATA events.

Later that same day, Dick had signed up for the handicap event. When he arrived at his starting field, he discovered he and Don Carlson were on the same squad.

At first, they didn't address each other at all. By the third round they had broken the ice and were having a civil conversation.

By the end of the day, they started a friendship that grew and remained close until Don's untimely death in 2017.

I have a very vivid and enjoyable memory of sitting in the beer tent at Vandalia, with Dick, Don, and Don's wife, Judy, while they re-enacted their first interaction at Las Vegas years before.

It was a warm and sunny afternoon following the day's events. Tears and laughter at its very best as both Dick and Don proved to be masters of storytelling.

Some things just can't be replaced.

Dick Marascola

Don Carlson

RUSS McCLENNAN

It's difficult to describe such a unique personality as Russ McClennan. He was the premier host for Harrah's at Lake Tahoe, entertaining high rollers from all over the globe.

As Vice-President of Player Development, Russ set up elaborate hunting and fishing trips for Harrah's clients and accompanied them on these endeavors.

"It's a tough job, but somebody has to do it" he once told me.

Following the Texas State Shoot in 1997, John Hall and I made a last-minute decision to fly to Alaska for a few days without so much as a single plan.

After landing in Anchorage, we rented a car and drove south to Soldotna. We checked into a motel and walked over to a nearby restaurant for dinner.

While there, a group of about ten walked in, and among them was Russ. He came over and visited with us for a bit, explaining this was a group of Harrah's customers, made up mostly of $5 slot players. You could tell he truly enjoyed his job.

Russ was also a trap shooter and became Nevada's ATA State Delegate in the early 90s. He worked side by side with Central

Handicap Committee Chairman, Dick Marascola, and spent many hours assisting shooters during major western tournaments, and at the Grand American at Vandalia, OH. He was an office staff favorite as he arrived every morning with pastries and donuts for the crews.

Russ and Dick also hosted a big party for many years during Grand week, cooking fresh foil-wrapped & buttered halibut on an outside grill, along with corn on the cob and fresh tomatoes. Hundreds dropped by to enjoy their hospitality.

I once stayed at his home in Stateline, overlooking Lake Tahoe. This was in June during the Nevada State Shoot. His home was a gorgeous place. Clint Eastwood and Jerry Van Dyke both had homes in the same area. The bedroom I stayed in featured a huge window with a panoramic view of the lake and surrounding mountains.

Every morning Russ would come up to wake me and bring coffee.

On the last day of the tournament, Russ came in, threw open the drapes and said- "It's a different view out there today". I sat up in bed and could see nothing but white.

Snow had covered everything and was coming down heavily. There was over 8" on the ground and it was June 13th. He told me the hotel often postponed golf tournaments for a day or two, due to unexpected snowfall, even in July.

Driving down Kingsbury Grade that morning to Genoa, we left the snow behind by the time we reached the Little Mondeaux Gun Club.

Russ and I became very good friends and I always looked forward to seeing him come to Las Vegas for our events.

The Rio Suite Hotel & Casino was a popular hotel host and we looked forward to returning there for our Fall Trapshooting Tournament in 1995. We invited all shooters, spouses and guests to a complimentary dinner and awards presentation in one of their elaborate ballrooms on Saturday night of the tournament.

A couple of days prior to this, Russ disappeared off the face of the earth, totally unannounced.

Obviously, I was very concerned and had calls made to the Las Vegas Metropolitan Police Department and all area hospitals. Russ was not to be found.

This was cause for great concern and weighed heavily on my mind as I prepared to address the crowd prior to presenting awards in the Rio's ballroom Saturday evening.

I was standing at the podium when suddenly approached by a hotel hostess. She extended her arm and I covered the microphone as I took the note from her hand.

Due to the events of the past two days I was expecting bad news.

Scribbled on a piece of tablet paper was the following, "Don't pay the ransom, I escaped".

I looked up to see Russ waving at me as he sheepishly entered the room and proceeded towards the back.

I didn't ask, and finally decided I didn't even want to know.

We lost Russ much too early in July 2003, at the age of 67.

If you're ever visiting Harrah's at Lake Tahoe, be sure to drop in the sports bar that bears his name and offer a special toast to this most deserving gentleman.

McLennan's Sports Bar, Harrah's Lake Tahoe

IRVING GOLDSTEIN

I would be neglectful should I not dedicate a section of this compilation to Irving Goldstein.

I had not been acquainted with Irv prior to my visit to the Las Vegas Gun Club's Fall 1987 Tournament. As mentioned in an earlier section, he later approached me about the possibility of buying out his lease to the property, and this same discussion continued for almost two years until we finally came to terms. Irv was a pawnbroker with a family-run pawnshop in Tucson.

After he obtained the 20-year lease of the gun club property in 1986, he was into it about 18 months when he began to feel the strain. He was taking time away from his family and primary business to be in Las Vegas.

He had hired a local part-time manager in Bill Mann, but the gun club was becoming a distraction. I asked why he had become interested in it at all. He said- "You know, I just always enjoyed coming to Las Vegas for the shoots."

After I obtained the lease from Irv, I remembered telling him- "Well maybe you'll enjoy coming back to the shoots now that it will no longer be work-related." He agreed.

On Friday, April 28, 2000, Irv, and passenger Allen Futrell (ATA shooter formerly of IL) rented a plane from a flying club of which Irv belonged, and flew from Tucson to Las Vegas to attend the 3rd North American Handicap Championship. Irv was the pilot. I had known Allen for many years and had purchased a live-bird gun from him during a program at Don Holford's place 20 years prior.

I was in the middle of conducting the tournament and remember it was extremely windy that day.

During the course of running the program, I was in and out of the clubhouse, and noticed breaking news coverage of a plane crash at the North Las Vegas airport coming through on one of the TVs over the bar.

I didn't think too much about it until another Tucson shooter mentioned that Irv and Allen were supposed to fly up that day.

I dropped what I was doing and called Russ Shoemaker, a club member, trap shooter and a detective with Las Vegas Metro. Russ could make inquiries for me regarding the crash scene as information was scarce.

About 30 minutes went by and Russ called me back. He said he had talked to officers on the scene and all they could confirm was there were shotgun shells scattered everywhere amongst the wreckage. I remember the extreme, sinking feeling that come over me.

From witness statements, apparently Irv had aborted two landing attempts in the extreme crosswinds. On the third attempt, he managed to set the plane down, but it immediately flipped over and burst into flames. There were no survivors and there was nothing anyone could do.

At some point I called the Coroner's Office for information, but they had nothing for me. I left them my name and number.

Thirty minutes or so later I was paged into the clubhouse for a phone call. It was Irv's son, Michael. Irv was supposed to have called his family once they arrived in Las Vegas. They had heard about the crash, but not heard from Irv. I told his son that I was aware of the crash, but nothing had been confirmed. I would let him know for sure once I had received news.

Not long after that, I received a phone call from the Coroner's Office, asking if I could come down to help with an identity. I dreaded this task but knew it was necessary.

Once at the Coroner's Office, they provided me with the Driver's License for both occupants lost in the crash. It was Irv and Allen; their license had survived the fire and were easily readable.

I had to call Irv's son back with the horrible news.

In the weeks to follow I often felt somewhat responsible for this tragic event. Obviously, had I not been hosting this new event, they would not have made the effort to come.

It took a while to get over this. Any personal setbacks I had experienced were minor; now & then life experiences are put into perspective.

Irv was 59; Allen was 52.

THE LONE STAR STATE

1997, 1998, & 1999 Texas State Trapshooting Championships

In 1996, I was asked by fellow shooter and ATA Texas State Delegate, Neal Crausbay, if I would consider hosting the 1997 Texas State Championships at the Permian Basin Shotgun Range. This club was located in West Texas between Midland and Odessa, and the tournament would be during the second week of July.

I was honored just to be asked so took the offer quite seriously. Within a few weeks I flew to Dallas and met with their State Association's directors and came to an agreement.

There would be much to do, especially the first year. A large portion of the trophies, staffing, training, target and ammunition procurement, advertisements, and program development, just to name a few. It's a big enough job to do at home, let alone doing it a thousand miles away in an area I was unfamiliar with.

I made the long drive after Memorial Day in 1997 and started pulling everything together. I had coordinated with the directors in the previous months to assure programs were already written, printed and mailed, and the advertising was out. Most of the trophies that were my responsibility were ordered from a local shop through phone calls and faxes.

One of my main concerns was the condition of the equipment I would have to work with. This was still in the time of the Western handset trap machines and manual pull cords. The Texas State Trapshooting Association had a few machines they provided; the rest were property of the Permian Basin club.

Plus, I had received information from a few Texas shooters that had experienced equipment problems when attending this club in the past. I decided it would be in my best interest to bring along my own trap mechanic, Randy Chambers. Randy made the trip down a couple of weeks prior to the tournament to start going through everything.

The club needed a few cosmetic improvements. There were eighteen trap fields in all, plus 4 of those were trap/skeet combination fields.

I reached out to long-time Missouri friend and shooter, Eddie Schneider, and told him I needed a hand. Eddie obliged, brought his 5th wheel and stayed on the grounds while painting every trap house, skeet house and the rail fence. I also had Britt Robinson come over and spend some time on the tractor mowing.

The tournament started without a hitch, but it wasn't long before I began hearing of some problems down on the east end.

Several fields were experiencing too many delayed, or no pulls. Randy had gone through all the trap machines and release cords assuring that everything had tested perfectly.

I finally went into one of the troublesome trap houses and stayed with the target setter while the squad continued shooting. I expected to hear a tell-tale buzz coming from the trap machines solenoid. This usually indicated low power or a micro-switch out of adjustment. This never happened.

Looking around inside the trap house, I noticed something unusual. There was a junction box on the back wall of the trap house that had a line going from it to the trap machine release cord receptacle. On the outside wall of the trap house facing the shooters was another receptacle. The release cord was plugged into this then extended back to the scorekeeper. I decided to bypass these junction boxes altogether and plugged the release cord directly into the machine. The problem was solved.

I found out later that several of the trap fields on the east end were subject to flooding, easily explaining the problems experienced while using the junction boxes.

The Amarillo Gun Club was in line to host the 1998 State Championships, and the facility was without a manager at the time. I was asked again if I would consider coming back to Texas and host their state championship program. I agreed.

Not long after accepting the proposal, I was contacted by Paulette Kirksey. Paulette and husband Benny were both long-time Texas trap shooters and supporters of the Amarillo club. They also owned a beloved Old English Sheep Dog by the name of Windsor.

Windsor was getting on in years and Paulette wanted to do something special for him, such as naming an event after him in the program. They would provide the trophies and $7500 in added money.

We wanted to do something special and called upon local shooters Bill and Joyce Dunlap. Bill and Joyce were providing many of the trophies that year, and both were being inducted into the Texas Trapshooting Hall of Fame. It was decided to create a likeness of Windsor to appear on several custom belt buckles for the event.

A couple of weeks later, we had the artwork, and I was elated with the results, as was Paulette. The resemblance to Windsor was uncanny. Champion, each yardage group winner, and yardage group runner-up would receive custom sterling belt buckles in the "Windsor Handicap" featuring Windsor himself in 18 kt. gold.

The remaining 1998 inductee into the Texas Hall of Fame was Gary Sherrod. Gary broke a 99 in the Windsor Handicap, but settled for the yardage buckle after losing to junior shooter Eric Ardeel in shoot-off. (Gary went on to win Sunday's Handicap Championship with another 99). The buckles came out perfect and became the most revered awards of the 1998 Texas State Championships.

A Texas-style awards presentation and party followed the Windsor event with Paulette awarding the buckles.

WINDSOR

I would return to Texas one more time as State Tournament Host in 1999 at the Permian Basin facility. Troy Collier offered to provide his 5th wheel for me to stay in for the month preceding the tournament. He brought the RV over 270 miles from Wichita Falls and set it up for me! A true friend indeed. Troy and his crew also prepared and served all the great food that week. His business of over 25 years, "Texas Best Meats" sells some of the finest meats and sauces to be found anywhere and is available online.

I enjoyed hosting all three of the Texas State Championships and managed to persuade Don Black to accompany me for all three. The photos from the tournaments are property of the Texas State Trapshooting Association.

Don Black

Don Black, San Carlos, CA, was a fixture for many years at the Las Vegas Gun Club, circa 1992-2001. Occasionally he was accompanied by his wife, Rose.

Don was a Pearl Harbor survivor and made the annual trip to Honolulu many times for reunions with former WWII shipmates. He passed in January 2011.

He was a crowd favorite as our own photographer and journalist, submitting photos and shoot reports for the Midwinter and Fall Trapshooting Tournaments, along with several additional programs that included the North American Handicap Championships and Silver State Open. Don enjoyed visiting with everyone, taking their photos and kissing the girls when they won something.

He and Dick Marascola were notorious for playing pranks on one another (It was a Pacific International Trapshooting Association vs Amateur Trapshooting Association thing). Don was a past PITA President, inducted into the PITA Hall of Fame in 2002, and Dick was the ATA Central Handicap Committee Chairman for many years, and inducted into the Trapshooting Hall of Fame in 2017.

Don provided detailed shoot reports which also included his own personal assessments of what was happening around the facility at the time of the tournament.

One day I came into the clubhouse from outside, and there was Don and Rose, both sitting behind the trophy table, and both sound asleep. I should have taken a photo myself.

Towards the end of this publication are the attendance numbers reflected in Don's reports, plus some of his personal notes, written verbatim. Any statements depicted in quotations are in Don's own words.

Don Black was an absolute pleasure to have at our facility for a period spanning over ten years. Many never-before-seen photos of past champions taken exclusively by Don are included at the very end of this publication. Complete tournament reports can be found in shooting publication archives.

Don Black, San Carlos, CA

Since Don began covering major trapshooting events at the Las Vegas Gun Club in September of 1992, that's where his shoot reports will begin! Please see the very end of the book for Don's reports and his professional portraits of Las Vegas Champions.

NEVADA'S HISTORICAL IMPACT ON TRAPSHOOTING TOURNAMENTS

The Smith family in Reno and the Del Webb Corporation in Las Vegas realized the potential new customer base to be nurtured among tournament trap shooters. Many were World War II survivors, and gamblers with a gusto for life. Harold's Club in the north, and the Flamingo and Sahara Hotel & Casino in the south marketed heavily in the 1950s and 1960s to bring the shooters to their respective locations.

Elaborate programs that awarded new Cadillacs, Ford Thunderbirds and other fine automobiles were the norm for the early days. The ladies in attendance were invited by the host hotel to lavish luncheons, bingo parties, fashion shows, and drawings for mink stoles and other valuable prizes. Slot tournaments and evening drawings for racks of silver dollars were common. I have copies of many of the Las Vegas programs, often featuring guest rooms for $12.00, and you could expect a couple of trips to the buffet or coffee shop in your guest package.

It wasn't only Reno and Las Vegas. Elko was also in on the action offering the "Baby Grand", just prior to the Golden West Grand in Reno. Like Reno and Las Vegas, Elko's events promised thousands of dollars in added money, guaranteed purses, cocktail parties and fun for all in attendance. The entire State of Nevada was onboard.

The word quickly spread amongst trap shooters around the entire country and Nevada's major trapshooting events grew rapidly.

The Flamingo Hotel served as shooters headquarters and hosted the Las Vegas Mid-Winter Trapshooting Tournament February 8-12, 1956. The guest package included a cocktail party on Thursday evening and a Trophy Dinner and floor show on Friday evening. For the trapshooting tournament they threw in $7,500 in Added Money and $6,875 in Guaranteed Purses. This was substantial in 1956. The tournament was co-sponsored by the Horseshoe Club and Golden Nugget.

This was the first Las Vegas Mid-Winter tournament I've been able to document. Over 450 attended. The tournament report was taken from "Pull" magazine as "Trap & Field" was still about 14 months away from being introduced and published.

Three months later, in May 1956, Harold's Club hosted its fifth Golden West Grand featuring almost $15,000 in Added Money, and $11,500 in Guaranteed Purses in the final two handicap events. At the time this was touted as the richest trapshooting tournament in the country. Targets in the GWG program were $6.50 per 100.

Fast forward a few years. Harold's Club is now hosting tournaments in Reno in March and May. Las Vegas is hosting events in February and September. The north and south ends of the State are competing with each other, and both are advertising the richest trapshooting tournaments in the West. Bob Taylor's Ranch House Gun Club (Las Vegas) has now been added into the mix and hosting a major January tournament. Along with these events, the Nevada State Trapshooting Championships are growing and alternating between the north and south each year. The 1962 Nevada State Shoot was held at Harold's Club alongside a 100-bird flyer (pigeon) shoot! Flyer tournaments were still openly advertised during this period.

The Desert Inn hosted the Las Vegas Midwinter Tournament in 1965. In addition to $7200 Added Money, and $7200 in Guaranteed Purses, the D.I. awarded the shooter with the high score on the final 200 handicap targets a brand new, completely loaded Pontiac GTO.

As a youngster growing up in Kansas City at this time, I would hear exciting reports from our locals that had travelled to Las Vegas and Reno. In this era, there simply was no other place like Nevada for trapshooting.

I was at the Sahara Gun Club in February 1967 when almost 1200 shooters attended. In the final handicap during a windstorm, Dan Orlich broke the only 25-straight on the first trap. If I remember correctly the payout was over $1200 just for the 25. This was part of the allure of Nevada. Big payoffs; but be prepared for big weather.

Unfortunately, the weather, particularly for the Mid-Winter and Spring Tournaments, took its toll, and attendance subsided and eventually dropped. Many clubs have come, and gone, from the Silver State in a period spanning almost fifty golden years.

On Saturday, December 19, 2009, Stef Carmichael fired the last shot at the Las Vegas Gun Club (previously the Flamingo, Stardust, Sahara & Mint)

On Saturday, August 31, 2013, Dan Orlich fired the last shot at the Sage Hill club in Reno, last site of the Golden West Grand in Nevada. My son was there beginning his last year in college and was able to attend. Both Dan and Stef are pictured below holding the empty casings of their historic final shots.

Dan Orlich and Stef Carmichael

END OF THE BIG SHOOT ERA AT LVGC

Following year after year of inclement weather impacting major trapshooting events at the Las Vegas Gun Club, I made the decision in late 2001 to back away from hosting large trap events and further diversify the facility. I would miss having the large trap events and the many shooters that enjoyed them and supported us, but a new game plan would be necessary for the business to survive in the coming years.

The Midwinter 2001 tournament was weather impacted to the point we would be late getting payoffs out to all our participants. I had pre-paid for an extra carload of targets and thousands of dollars of ammunition that went unused. Equipment leases, printing costs, tournament cashiers, and tournament staff still had to be paid in full. I had the inventory, but not the cash.

I sent letters out to everyone letting them know it would take us at least an extra month to resolve everything. In lieu of this, A California shooter that was owed $200 filed an official complaint to the ATA. This was his right and perfectly according to the rules.

Soon, I received a letter from Bob Melton, Secretary of the ATA, that I was suspended. My conduct, according to Mr. Melton was "reprehensible." No participation allowed in ATA events, and no hosting of ATA events until everything resolved. I didn't know it at the time, but this turned out to be a blessing.

Even though everything was cleared up by April, I decided to pass on having the Annual Fall Tournament in September.

As it turned out, this tournament would have been seriously impacted following the devastating 9/11 attack in New York. This certainly would have resulted in another financial setback. After over 40 years in the ATA, it had come down to this.

This situation had been building for a couple of years. I refused to give away sub-par prizes. My mindset had always been if you came to Las Vegas, you would win silver, gold, guns, ammo, and possibly automobiles. Trophy/prize budgets often exceeded $35,000 for a major tournament. In turn, it was assumed the shooters would participate. I overlooked the possibility they may not do so, and this cost me dearly.

Every event required a minimum number of shooters to break even; there's no making it up on the next event. I realized I had become a dinosaur in the game and not in tune with the majority of current shooter's needs at all.

I was of the old school, and another era. Proof was provided in several instances when we offered valuable prizes to be won, yet shooters would often sit out the events if conditions deteriorated. Unfortunately, deterioration of weather was a common factor in Las Vegas during the month of February. Weather had played a major role in eight of the eleven Midwinter Tournaments we hosted from 1990 until 2001.

Another perfect case study was the North American Handicap Championship; offered in late April; 1998, 1999, & 2000. At the top of the prize list were automobiles; guaranteed, followed by other valuable prizes and custom buckles.

The first year of these three programs the event lost about $5,000. I considered that acceptable for a launch of a new and innovative event. I tweaked a couple of things before the second year. It worked, as attendance jumped 40% and the tournament produced net revenues of about $7,000. However, the identical program the third year resulted in attendance dropping about 20%. I wasn't too concerned at first as this could have been due to a change of the host hotel or possible conflict with another event. This would have still been negligible financially, but winds came in Friday and Saturday, and event participation fell through the floor.

Three hundred thirty-one shooters had registered and only 83 shooters participated in Saturday morning's handicap. Bottom line, over $5,000 was lost on the third tournament and we realized that continuing such a program in the future would be foolhardy. Even for this type of prize-heavy program, many shooters would no longer participate if conditions were less than desirable.

I now realized for the past eleven years I had made the mistake of presenting programs that would have been to my own liking as a competitor in the 1970s. Times had changed, and my lesson had been painfully learned. I finally realized, no matter what the prizes may be, our ATA shooters had become older and appeared they were there more to socialize and participate rather than to win something of value. Furthermore, they wanted to shoot in comfort and not fight the elements. I would likely do the same at this stage of my life.

By this time, Las Vegas hotels & casinos had lost interest in sponsoring and hosting large trap events, claiming this was no longer a gambling group. I don't know if this was true or not. Hotels were reluctant to discount rooms for events that took guests away from the property for most of the day. It was noticeable that resort hotels were becoming more corporate and increasingly difficult to deal with on a personal level. If guests were not using new I.D. cards provided by the hotel for tracking gambling activity, there was really no way to know if the trapshooting groups were gambling or not. There was no friendly interaction between shooting guests and shift managers, or pit bosses as there had been in the past. There was no doubt the age of the average ATA shooter may have played a role in this; they had been there and done that in times past.

I was at the point I no longer wanted the temptation of hosting a major trapshooting event again without major hotel/casino financial support. Times were changing in the ATA. Satellite Grands had now gained strength in numbers and received the lion's share of promotion and coverage. Hosting a Satellite Grand also required a large payment to the ATA up front to procure the event. We had already suffered major financial setbacks during several of our largest trap tournaments which resulted in refinancing and need for a new business plan. We decided to go a different, and safer direction based on sound business principles.

The entire Las Vegas Gun Club property was on only 78 acres. There were no additional areas to develop new venues. This resulted in a need for major re-configuration of existing fields.

We would add skeet and sporting clays to appeal to a broader spectrum of customers. Local shooters Art Curtis and Cadry Genena had proposed building an International Trap bunker on the property. They would build, supply and run the bunker. All I had to do was provide the space. There was an ideal location just east of the new skeet fields where the ground dropped down about ten feet to a lower elevation. This was perfect as it allowed the bunker to be accessed easily on the east end with large doors. Pallets of targets could be rolled into the bunker from this point.

I requested, and received, from my landlord, approval to remove 16 of the existing trap fields. Six of these fields on the far east end were already in poor condition, plus several of them faced straight west and were unusable in the afternoon. These fields had been constructed quickly just prior to the 1985 Supershoot hosted by Bob Taylor.

The lower end of the property was re-designed and became a 10-station sporting clays course. Two concrete-block skeet fields and the International bunker were built just to the east of the clubhouse. A new promotion was launched, and we were able to garner 500 family memberships within a few months plus a new following of local and diversified shotgunners. This would provide the financial stability needed for the remaining portion of our lease.

Local participation, league activity and overall usage of the facility increased dramatically. We still held ATA events, but on a much smaller scale involving zero risk. The remaining fourteen trap fields were perfect for this.

After eleven years, I was finally achieving stability and peace of mind. I would never again worry about what the weather forecast may be, where riots may be occurring, terrorists may be attacking, or anything else that was beyond my control.

Custom .999 silver bars up to 64 ounces
Bars & boxes created by Bill Mains,
Mains Enterprises, Inc.

THE FUTURE OF REGISTERED TRAPSHOOTING?

The sport of registered trapshooting has evolved to the point in the last five decades it's hardly a remnant of its former self. From the beginning, trapshooting was a money sport based on rules that assured fair competition. Many former live pigeon shooters made the crossover to clay target shooting for ethical, practical and/or financial reasons. I believe it would be fair to say 75-90% of the competitors in major trapshooting tournaments during the 1950s and 60s entered all the purses and options available. The lure of a financial windfall for a good performance attracted an abundance of then twenty-somethings and middle-aged shooters alike.

I can easily identify a group of a fifteen 27-yard shooters that emerged by the late 70s that would be responsible for many changes in ATA tournaments, simply due to their consistent performances in handicap events. This entire group dedicated themselves to major trapshooting tournaments as either their primary or supplemental income. They were talented, plus competing more than ever before, and becoming better along the way. Open purses and options began to lose their appeal as short and mid-yardage shooters believed they may be able to compete with one or two of the top gunners, but not all of them. This led to the demise of the open purse & options and rise of the yardage purse and Lewis Class. The ATA was under pressure to do something about this, but uncertain what the correct step would be.

Along with this, the ATA was finding itself in an identity crisis. What started as the Interstate Trapshooting Association in 1890, became the American Trapshooting Association in 1919, and finally the Amateur Trapshooting Association in 1923. By true definition, those participating in amateur sports are not to receive monetary compensation. Early on, the ATA designated an "Industry" class for ammunition and firearms representatives, but that was about as far as they were willing to go identifying professionals. This new group of top shooters mentioned above were also becoming involved in teaching, and other industry related money-making ventures that would clearly label them as professionals. The ATA just didn't know what to do with them.

By the time the 1980s rolled around, many trap clubs were beginning to throw less difficult targets to appeal to a broader audience. It's human nature to return to a facility where you've performed well on prior visits. The problem with this; clubs were no longer comparing apples-to-apples with regards to target settings.

There's a tremendous amount of difference in a clay target thrown a distance 48-49 yards on a trap field versus one that is thrown 51-52 yards. The faster target is exponentially unforgiving and requires a perfect movement by the shooter to achieve positive results from the longer yardages. Only seasoned shooters were aware of this. As a result, they dedicated many hours to improving their game and equipment to achieve success.

Finally, a reduction of target angle became the norm, and everyone was competitive again. Or, so they thought. Now, instead of the top shooters winning handicap events with 97 or 98, they're entering 99s and 100s on a regular basis. The average shooter is registering better scores but may be even less competitive than they were before. The serious money has left the ATA once and for all and will not return.

As mentioned earlier, this appeared to be the goal of at least one of our prior Executive Committee members thirty years ago, possibly rightfully so when considering the true meaning of amateur. The expansion of recognized special categories and downgrading of trophies to allow almost everyone to receive an award was another potentially risky venture. If this is successful or not is still to be determined. More events have been added to make up for individual entry shortfall. I fear we have applied band-aid over band-aid in attempt to stop the bleeding.

Trapshooting is not a spectator sport in its present form. As such, it will never draw major advertisers and/or sponsors. Any money to be won will have to be generated from the contestants except for an occasional local sponsor or club added money. However, the ATA might be able to serve as a stepping-stone that competitors could go through to reach higher levels of competition if they chose to do so.

Perhaps consider a branch of the ATA referred to as ATA+. This would amount to no more than tournaments with different target settings and a different set of record-keeping requirements. I've listed some considerations below for ATA+ regarding target settings for 16 yard and handicap events-

- Targets thrown not less than 51 yards nor more than 53 yards in calm air or set to the speed by a certified device that correlates to these distances

- Target maximum right angle not less than a straightway from post 1

- Target maximum left angle not less than a straightaway from post 5

I don't believe the average ATA shooter realizes the degree of difficulty these very simple changes create; it's massive. As in most cases "speed kills" and this is no exception when it comes to long yardage shooters. These types of target settings are much more difficult for seasoned, experienced shooters than they are for the average shooter. More inexperienced shooters may not even be aware of such a change, but they will notice the drop of scores overall. Especially from the 27-yard line.

Other considerations for ATA+

- Each field requires a scorekeeper and qualified referee

- Enforcement of a "No Balk Rule"

*No balk rule- *If a whole target appears on the shooter's command and a failure to shoot for any reason, the target is scored "lost".*

Many of you are probably wondering why even consider this. My answer is- to stimulate the game, and possibly the entire industry. The type of target settings described above will almost certainly result in equipment modifications or changes altogether. The natural response of the shooter needs to be in perfect tune with the target flight and angle, not just close, to obtain good results from handicap yardages. The handicap system might just begin working once again.

To advance the ATA+ concept, there's no doubt the organization would need to sweeten the pot to promote it. Guaranteed purse minimums might be effective, or perhaps even recruit new sponsors willing to lend their name to purse guarantees or prizes. A great deal hinges on current beliefs of the ATA; would they rather all money truly be eliminated from the game, or not. If they choose the latter, then an entirely new spin-off organization would be required to develop clay target competitions for substantial cash or prize awards.

For this reference I'll propose the designation of American Clay Pigeon, or ACP. Qualifications would be unnecessary, and competitors could compete back and forth between ACP and ATA program structures at will. However, equipment changes or modifications in the trap house would be necessary. The good news is that as few as four or eight existing regulation trap fields would allow a small club to host some very lucrative events. Keep in mind, modern day trapshooting was derived <u>directly</u> from live pigeon shooting. Advancements in technology now provide us the ability to throw a clay target that more closely resembles the flight of a live bird. I've confirmed this with a well-known trap manufacturer several years ago during the SHOT Show here in Las Vegas. I would propose that a tournament structure for the ACP level of competition would include the following-

- Targets to be thrown at variable speeds, 45-55 yards, speed/distance unknown to the shooter at time of call based on cam position (achievable)

- Targets with possibility of wider angles at departure (easily obtainable)

- Targets with possibility of varying heights (easily obtainable)

- Targets with possibility of varying attitudes (left or right lean; achievable)

- Mandatory purses and options; one flat entry fee per event

- No Balk Rule

- 75-target events including purse, two 50s, three 25s & Lewis Class

- 2-shot events from 22 yards, 1-shot events from handicap yardage with a minimum of 22 yards.

- Each field requires a scorekeeper and qualified referee

Such tournaments have the potential to develop spectator appeal. There is an element of luck based on what target the shooter draws and 25-straights would be rare. Serious prize money would be generated, appealing to a new and large group of individuals without the ATA sacrificing its role or identity. Smaller clubs could be brought into the fold as nothing is required but four regulation trap fields equipped with modified traps. One field for practice, three fields for events. There is potential of breathing life back into the smaller four-trap facilities with such a program.

Events would be made up of two-shot and single-shot events daily to bring everyone into the fold. Live pigeon, helice, sporting clays, skeet and trap shooters would all be represented in such events. Two prelim days with two 75-bird events each day, followed by identical main day programs on Saturday and Sunday with increased purses and options.

Luck must play a role to be successful. Every year, thousands of card players descend upon Las Vegas for the World Series of Poker. The majority of these are between 25 and 30 years old, each forking up $10,000 to play in the main event. If skill alone was involved, I doubt there would be 250 entrants. This group has no interest in competing for participation awards. It's the excitement of the big money and recognition that drives everything. In the ACP trap program, the very next target launched could be a "maker" or "breaker".

An ACP program may look something like below-

Thursday- Prelim Day 1

Event 1- 75-Target 2-Shot Event

Entry.. $135

Entry includes $5 on each of three 25s, divided 60-40%

$10 on each of two 50s, divided 50-30-20%

$25 on total purse, divided 40-30-20-10%

$25 Lewis Class, (4) divided 60-40% each

Event 2- 75-Target 1-Shot Event

Entry, purse & option structure same as Event 1

Friday Prelim Day 2

Event 3 & 4; Repeat Thursday

Awards on the Preliminary 300 Targets

Open Champion, Runner-Up & Third

Lady Champion, Runner-Up & Third

Senior Champion (over 65), Runner-Up & Third

Saturday- Main Day 1

Event 5- 75-Target 2-Shot Event

Entry..$195

Entry includes $10 on each of three 25s, divided 60-40%

$20 on each of two 50s, divided 50-30-20%

$50 on total purse, divided 40-30-20-10%

$25 Lewis Class, (4) divided 60-40% each

Event 6- 75-Target 1-Shot Event

Entry, purse & option structure same as Event 5

Sunday- Main Day 2

Event 7 & 8; Repeat Saturday

Awards on the Main 300 Targets

Open Champion, Runner-Up & Third

Lady Champion, Runner-Up & Third

Senior Champion (over 65), Runner-Up & Third

The entry fee on all events leave $50 per entry to apply to the cost of targets, cashiering & labor costs, plus leaves enough for the limited number of awards to be substantial. Most importantly, the host club will realize a profit and be eager to host future events. Without financial health of our local clubs, all will certainly be lost in the not-so-distant future.

I would like to believe introduction of the tournament structure described above would not only bolster a new and exciting aspect of trapshooting, but also boost participation in the ATA.

The ATA is having tremendous success bringing young shooters into ATA events, plus have a reasonably strong contingency of Vet and Sr. Vets. It's the post-junior and middle-age group that is missing. It's also likely that many of the youngsters will go in a different direction and abandon trapshooting once they're on their own. Being responsible for their own shooting costs with little return may not appeal to many. Perhaps they will return much later in life, but this doesn't solve the large gap currently between junior-age and senior-age participants.

If I were twenty years younger, I might attempt to bring this to fruition but at this point in my life, I would hope that someone else will show interest and take on the task.

JUST ONE OF THOSE TOWNS

Las Vegas is one of those places that anyone may drop into at any time. Over the years I've experienced many encounters that had nothing to do with trapshooting but provided memorable moments none the less.

I owned a 1985 Porsche 928S for several years in the early 1990s and enjoyed it immensely on the sparsely populated highways of Nevada. Traveling to Elko or Reno was enjoyable instead of mundane, and at times, 170+ mph was indicated on the speedometer. The 928S was equipped with a front-mounted, 350 hp water-cooled 32-valve overhead cam engine. It was built specifically for the German Autobahn and increased in stability as it accelerated. Somehow, the car just magically became flatter and wider at high speeds. It also weighed 3500 pounds which was heavy for a Porsche.

After two or three years of this I decided I had better sell it before a coyote or something else crossed the road in front of me ending in catastrophic results.

I finally advertised the car in the newspaper and within a day or two received a phone call from a prospective buyer. I was behind the counter of the gun club at the time and invited the caller to come out that afternoon. From the club we would drive down to the house where the car was parked in the garage.

An hour or so later, a gentleman walked through the door and introduced himself as Richard. We chatted a bit then he rode with me down to my residence.

I pulled the car out of the garage and we ended up on Highway 95 headed north. I let Richard drive while he explained he had just gone through a bad divorce and had recently returned to Las Vegas after several years in Florida.

We eventually drove back to the house and parked the car. He said he believed he was more in the market for a model that was a little lighter on the front end such as the 911. However, he said he would be very interested in joining the Las Vegas Gun Club. He enjoyed shooting and wanted to bring his grandson out and introduce him to the clay target sports.

I brought him into the house and introduced him to Lidia. We chatted a bit more, then he wrote out a check for the annual club membership. I drove him back up to the club. We shook hands and he left.

After I returned home that evening, I picked the check up off the counter and looked at it. "Smother's Brothers Productions" in the upper left-hand corner. Holy cow, that was Dick Smothers. I told Lidia. She said- "No it wasn't" to which I replied- "Yes it was."

When you're so used to seeing someone as part of a 2-person team you don't even recognize them when they're by themselves.

Dick and his grandson came out and shot with us many times and was always a pleasure to have around. I never knew if he found the Porsche he was looking for or not.

About a year later, once again I was behind the counter at the club and took a phone call from Barbara Mandrell's road manager. Barbara had an engagement at one of the hotels and would like to come out one day and shoot some trap with us. I said we would be delighted to have her and made tentative plans to have her come out the following Friday.

The Friday arrived and I was talking with several of our local customers that morning in the pro shop. I mentioned that Barbara Mandrell may be coming out to join us later in the day. A gentleman at the back of the room said- "Actually, she's not going to be able to make it out today. I'm her husband, Ken."

Ken Dudney and Barbara Mandrell became members of the club and shot with us many times when Barbara was in town. Barbara's younger sister, Irlene, also came out on several occasions and was involved with the "Make-A-Wish" Foundation. We hosted a Fall Tournament with the Rio Hotel to benefit the "Make-A-Wish" Foundation in 1996. Irlene served as our hostess for the event, which also featured a fabulous banquet and charity auction at the Rio Hotel.

Another occasion, same scenario, I received a call from a gentleman that identified himself only as "Jules", and stated that he was head of security in Las Vegas for the Prince of Brunei. The Prince was currently in Las Vegas and would like to shoot International Trap if possible. I explained to Jules that we couldn't provide an International Trap bunker but did have a wobble trap we could set up for him with advance notice. Jules also mentioned there would be a tremendous amount of security involved and that a field away from everyone else would be preferred if possible. I mentioned this would be no problem and we set a date for an upcoming Thursday afternoon.

I didn't know much about the Royal family of Brunei at the time, but I was about to find out.

A few days later, Thursday rolled around, and Jules called to say they were on their way and would arrive in a few minutes. What followed was amazing.

Four black Lincoln sedans rolled into the facility and parked in the area directly behind the designated shooting field. This was about 200' west of the clubhouse behind field #6. Two obvious security personnel jumped out of each vehicle and set up a perimeter that encompassed the entire field and parking area. About five minutes later, a white Mercedes limousine pulled in followed by four additional black Lincoln sedans. The white limo ended up surrounded by the black Lincolns on three sides. I noticed all the Lincolns were from the MGM Grand Hotel.

I discovered later that another black Lincoln had remained at the intersection where the gun club road split off from Durango Drive.

A designated attendant opened the rear door of the limo and the Prince emerged, also clad in white. It was at this time I was formally introduced to Prince Jefri Bolkiah, younger brother of the Sultan of Brunei. After doing some research later I discovered his formal name was much, much longer.

A temporary shade structure was erected. Rugs and folding chairs were placed under it. At least three coolers containing snacks and beverages were removed from one of the Lincoln's trunks and placed on the rug.

One attendant brought out the Prince's shooting vest, while the designated gun-bearer assembled an extremely high-grade Beretta SO series over/under and placed it in the gun rack.

I wasn't aware at the time, but the Prince was an accomplished bunker shooter and hosted International Trap events in his home country. He was also left-handed.

I introduced the two staff members that would be assisting him on the field; one loader and one puller/scorekeeper as this was before automatic traps and voice call systems.

Within a few minutes, the Prince walked out to station 1, and turned around. This was the cue for his gun-bearer to bring him the shotgun while another attendant brought ammunition. Everything was done very formally and precisely. He started his first round and I returned to the clubhouse at this point.

About 45 minutes had gone by and suddenly, everyone departed just as rapidly as they had arrived. Jules called me within a few minutes and explained something had come up and they had to leave immediately. He also said the Prince enjoyed himself and would like to return on the following Monday if possible. Monday was perfect for this type of guest as we were closed to the public on Monday and he would have the entire place to himself.

After I hung up the phone, I realized we could put on a nice spread of food for the Prince if we knew in advance what he liked. We had an excellent kitchen and chef at the club.

I had no contact phone number for Jules as he was calling our desk phone and there was no ID provided. I remembered the MGM identification on the Lincolns and allowed time for them to arrive back in town.

An hour later, I called the MGM and spoke with a receptionist. I told her who I was, and that I believed the Prince of Brunei was staying with them and I was trying to reach Jules, the Prince's head of security while in Las Vegas. She said- "Ah yes, they have the entire 26th floor of the hotel. I'll see if I can reach Jules and have him get back to you."

Thirty or so minutes later Jules called me back. He gave me a list of beverages and several things the Prince enjoyed eating. I assured him we'd have a nice surprise for him when he returned the following Monday.

When Monday rolled around, the entry process repeated itself with all the Lincolns and the white Mercedes. This time the Prince stayed for about four hours, shooting 200 targets, and taking breaks in the shade between rounds. There were four other family members with him along with the security personnel.

This time, when everyone left, Jules and the gun-bearer stayed behind. Jules came in to settle the bill, and stuck around for a while, in no apparent hurry to leave. We had a great opportunity to get to know each other and had a fascinating discussion.

I learned that Jules lived in Las Vegas, and the Prince of Brunei was his only client. When the Prince was inbound, Jules usually had a four to five-hour window to have all the local security needed in place. This seemed a daunting task.

The gun-bearer had a British accent. I asked him how does a Brit become the gun-bearer for the Prince of Brunei? He laughed and said he had applied for the position after being referred by an acquaintance of the family. He was retired from the British Army and felt this was the perfect retirement job.

Both men explained that the citizens of Brunei want for nothing, all is provided by the Royal Family. Brunei was often referred to as Shangri-La. I never considered that Shangri-La was an actual place and really existed. For obvious reasons, you must be invited to reside there.

I asked what had happened that led to the sudden departure the previous Thursday. Jules said they had to make a quick trip to Los Angeles for an appearance on Friday.

What was really interesting was they travelled in two separate Boeing 747's for the short Los Angeles trip. One plane included the Prince and eight family members, the other included the security team. The strategy was that outsiders wouldn't know which plane the Prince occupied.

I found out later the Prince was dealing with legal issues in the United States and the trip to Los Angeles may have been part of that. He had built a home in Henderson complete with Polo fields and paddocks, plus another home in Spanish Trails on twenty acres. As far as I know he never resided in either of these.

And, these were his only two visits to the Las Vegas Gun Club.

The Prince and the Sultan's extravagant lifestyles and legal issues have been well documented since Prince Jefri visited us. This was the wealthiest family in the world until Bill Gates amassed his fortune.

There's a plethora of jaw-dropping information to be found online regarding the Royal Family of Brunei.

***

We had many other interesting visitors over the years. Travis Tritt and his entire Country Club Band rolled in with their tour bus and shot with us on two occasions.

Renowned skateboarder Tony Hawk came by and shot with us, as did NBA great Karl "The Mailman" Malone, and NFL Oakland Raiders Quarterback, "The Mad Bomber", Daryle Lamonica. Daryle presented me with a signed painting of the famous 1968 "Heidi Game." For those unfamiliar, the Raiders scored two touchdowns against the New York Jets in the final minute of the game to win. This comeback happened immediately after NBC broke away from its game coverage on the East Coast to broadcast the television film "Heidi." Obviously, New York fans were livid. This changed the way NFL games were televised from that point forward.

For those of you that were early CBS "Survivor" fans, one of the first season, "Survivor: Borneo" stars, was Susan Hawk (unrelated to Tony). Her and husband Tim later moved to Las Vegas and spent several years with us as members and weekly visitors to the club. Sue was exactly the same personality you saw on TV, and as real as the day is long.

Susan's "snakes and rats" speech during the final Tribal Council of the first season has been cited as one of the greatest and most memorable speeches in the show's history. Susan presented us with a large collectible poster of her memorable speech.

Rick Dale was our neighbor up the street, and often had old iron stoves or other antiques he had restored for sale on the sidewalk in front of his home. He became well-known years later as the star of "American Restoration" appearing on the History Channel.

EPILOGUE

The last shot was fired at the Las Vegas Gun Club on Saturday, December 19, 2009. During our tenure of almost 19 years, a total of 40 million clays had been thrown at our facility. This was also the final chapter of a club that had served and hosted major trapshooting tournaments under the following names- The Flamingo, Sahara, Sahara-Mint, Mint, and Landmark Gun Clubs, spanning a period of over 60 years. It's likely that every top shooter in the country had competed there at one time or another.

Following the closing, I began the process of final lead reclamation and eventually total evacuation of the property. Trap machines were given a final once over, removed from their mounts, palletized and prepared for sale. Voice equipment was boxed up, left over targets, rental guns, & various accessories, all made ready for new owners. Same for the scoring stands, gun racks, benches, on-deck boards, steel storage containers, etc. This was a daunting task. In preparation of the property for final check-out by the City of Las Vegas, everything would need to be 100% complete and ship shape.

For obvious reasons, my main concern was the lead reclamation. Over the nineteen years of our occupancy, I had kept accurate records of prior lead shot recovery as this had the potential to become a major sticking point.

I called in a good friend, Bruce Kilen, to assist with the final clean-up. Bruce provided a skid steer, loader, grader and screen plant. I had a small but very efficient piece of equipment that all fines from the large screen plant would go through to produce our final product.

For several days Bruce used the grader, carving out wind rows oriented east-west, and traversing the entire shot drop area. These were collected with the loader and processed through the screen plant.

There was one area approximately one hundred and fifty yards in front of the clubhouse that turned into a wash during flash flooding following heavy rains. This area was about three hundred feet long and twenty feet wide. I was sure there had to be a considerable build-up of lead shot in this area as it had never been touched in prior clean ups. Bruce started with the grader at one end, scraping 3-4" deep with each pass. The lead shot could be seen easily as a dark streak in the sandy colored ground. Pass after pass after pass, and we were finally down about four feet before the dark streaks finally disappeared. For years, flood waters had allowed the lead shot to sink down further down into the ground. This one small concentrated cut produced over 20,000 pounds of lead shot in amazingly good condition.

There were a few delays in the reclamation process due to an extremely wet February. The final screening, shaking and blowing of the aggregate required the material be bone dry to result in a clean product. Final clean-up was completed in April, and all finished product sold and hauled off in May.

All in all, seventy-eight, fifty-five-gallon drums of clean lead shot were produced by the final clean-up. The drums averaged almost 3000 pounds each. More importantly, I had complete and detailed records indicating I had removed more lead shot than I had contributed to the property over our 19-year period of tenure.

On June 6, 2010, a representative from the City of Las Vegas met me at the facility for the final inspection and walk-through. He signed us off with flying colors and we locked up the entry gate for the final time. In some ways it felt as if I was leaving part of myself behind.

Approximately 18 months after the closing of the Las Vegas Gun Club, I was hired in February 2011 as administrator of the Clark County Shooting Complex. It took a while to adjust from a private business to a government entity. For over 19 years I had become accustomed to 60 to 70-hour weeks. Days off were rare, and weekends off were out of the question. Now, I was suddenly limited to working only 40 hours per week.

The Shooting Complex had opened the public module about 14 months before my arrival. Situated on 2880 acres, it was destined to be many years before achieving full build-out. Clark County was still suffering after-effects of the recession. As a result, one of the Commissioners had labeled the new facility as a money pit and was pushing for privatization. While built with funds generated by the sale of public lands in southern Nevada, operations were being funded by the taxpayers. The Shooting Complex was established as an Enterprise Fund and expected to generate enough revenue to be self-sufficient.

Necessary changes occurred slowly but surely, as we concentrated on additional venues to provide maximum revenues while cutting expenses. The original proformas were cast aside as we operated without a fully built-out facility.

One of the first duties I had to perform after being hired was the immediate layoff of three of our full-time positions. I hated this, but fortunately one of these was ready to retire, and the remaining two found new positions within different county departments.

Eventually, the Shooting Complex achieved break-even status and the pressure we had endured in the early years subsided.

I have an amazing and dedicated staff to work with and it's a pleasure to come to work each morning. Time seems to go by quickly these days, but I have been truly blessed to be where I am at this time.

The 2020 Grand American Trapshooting Championships were held at Linn Creek, Missouri, as the world dealt with the Covid-19 pandemic. The A.T.A. home grounds location at Sparta, IL, was not allowed to host the major event due to Covid-19 related restrictions in the State of Illinois.

Las Vegas has been hit particularly hard by this scourge as the city's economic engine is so dependent on tourism. Activity at the Shooting Complex, along with about everything else operated by Clark County, came to a screeching halt on Monday, March 16, 2020, following one of our busiest weekends ever. On March 17, our Governor announced a total shutdown of the entire state to begin March 19. On Friday, March 20, two thousand Clark County part-time workers were automatically terminated. Over 105 of those were assigned to the Shooting Complex as experienced Range Safety Officers, Range Masters, and Customer Service Representatives. It was a long and strenuous process to bring them back onboard when the time finally rolled around.

Eventually, we reopened on Friday, June 26, 2020, but public shooting was limited to three days and few hours due to insufficient staffing levels. Part of our staffing deficit was attributable to Covid-19, and part was due to CARES federal unemployment subsidy. It will be some time before we're back to normal.

Covid-19 has also struck very close to home. Long-time A.T.A. shooter, and past President of the Nevada State Trapshooting Association, Dean Shepardson, was hospitalized with the virus on July 6 and passed on July 21. He had been shooting at the Wyoming State Shoot on July 2. More recently, one of our long-time Camper Hosts, Bill Schmidt, died of Covid in November. Ron Lurie, a past Mayor of Las Vegas and senior member of our Advisory Committee succumbed to the virus three days before Christmas.

Two of our staff tested positive in January 2021, resulting in a 2-week closure of the public rifle/pistol center, and quarantine of those exposed. Fortunately, both staff members fully recovered, and no further outbreaks occurred.

My son now lives in Dallas, TX, and is a financial advisor for a major investment firm. He contracted the virus in June. He initially lost his sense of smell and taste, but otherwise felt fine. He continued to work at home and was void of all symptoms within two weeks of the onset. Unfortunately, many have not fared as well.

My daughter works for the State of Nevada Department of Corrections. She tested positive right after Christmas but recovered in just a few days after 48 hours of severe headaches.

Lidia and I have been extremely fortunate to have a home with a large yard, mature trees, and hedges. Time off during the pandemic has kept us busy working on the property and maintaining some sense of normalcy. I'm not sure how those living in apartments have done it. It's had to be extremely difficult.

One of the unexpected side effects of the pandemic was that Clark County placed all full-time staff on 4-day work weeks. This has allowed me an extra day to complete this publication that began almost three years ago.

In closing, it's my hope that everyone reading this has either experienced an enjoyable trip down memory lane, learned something of the history, or discovered a new appreciation for trapshooting in general.

The sport has changed a great deal over the last five decades, and those participating today will be responsible for how it fares in the future. Hopefully, some of the history presented here will be in their thoughts moving forward.

TEN YEARS OF MAJOR ATA LAS VEGAS TOURNAMENT RESULTS- IN THE WORDS OF DON BLACK

1992 Fall Tournament- September 22-27

"528 individual shooters came from 30 states and 3 Canadian Provinces to form 2766 entries and to fire at almost 263,000 targets in competition for fantastic silver and gold trophies."

"In addition to the hospitality provided by the Las Vegas Gun Club and the Aladdin Hotel, the shooters, and their families, were treated to:"
"A delicious Alaskan Salmon Bake dinner provided by the members of the Las Vegas Gun Club after the conclusion of the shooting on Preliminary Day."

"A Friday evening award ceremony, open to all shooters and their families, put on by the Aladdin Hotel. The Hotel provided tables brimming with hot Hors d'oeuvres and three fully staffed bars".

"The shooters were subjected to a wide variety of weather; everything from very hot and still to cool, strong winds. One day the wind would come from the south and the next day it would turn around and come from the north. As a result of the caliber of shooters present and the excellent setting and throwing of the targets, the scores were above average."

"All though there were many All Americans present, and 100 straights were not uncommon, one young shooter stood out. Mike Patterson started shooting registered trap on Feb. 23, 1992, at the 19-yard line. Twelve shoots later, on July 17, 1992, he earned his way to the 27-yard line! Mike won four trophies at this shoot! "

Note- Clay target replica awards provided are Bill Main's original, actual size and .99 pure silver. This grade of silver and sterling was used for all awards during the next 10 years of major trap event at the Las Vegas Gun Club. S.C.

Lidia and Steve Carmichael
Aladdin Hotel Awards Presentation 1992
1993 Mid-Winter Tournament- February 23 - 28

"Five hundred and forty shooters, representing 39 states and four Canadian Provinces, fired at well more than a quarter of a million targets attempting to win one, or more, of the sterling silver and gold trophies. The shoot was hosted by the Las Vegas Gun Club and the Aladdin Hotel. Other hosts, at this shoot, were SCOTTSHOT (Larry Scott and Bill Hunter), Dollar Rent A Car and Winchester Arms. Bill Hunter donated all of the Veteran and Senior Veteran trophies."

"Even though the weather, for the most part, was not favorable to the shooters, the scores for a winter shoot were well above average. The above average scores can be attributed to several factors; the caliber of the shooters participating, the condition of the traps (provided and maintained by Chuck Elton) and the performance of the Las Vegas pullers and setters under some very difficult conditions. There were 47 100 straights and two 200 straights in the 16 Yard Events and one100 straight in Doubles."

"Three complimentary cocktail parties were hosted by the Las Vegas Gun Club and the Aladdin Hotel. The highlight of the parties was the awarding of 100 silver dollars at each party. Each shooter, when registering for the shoot, was given free raffle tickets that were used in the $100 drawings."

1993 Fall Tournament- September 21-26

"Five hundred and forty-four shooter, representing 41 states, formed 2740 entries and fired at over a quarter million targets in an attempt to win one, or more, of the sterling silver and gold buckles and silver ingots that were provided as trophies. The shoot was hosted by the Las Vegas Gun Club and the Rio Suite Hotel."

"Excellent shooting conditions and properly maintained and operated traps resulted in some outstanding scores. A large portion of the country's outstanding trap shooters were present; however, three shooters stood out; Earl Scripture, Ross Warren and youngster Jeffrey Holguin. Earl broke every 16-yard target that he fired at including a 300-bird shoot-off between Earl and Ross in which the targets were made increasingly difficult by throwing wider, faster and lower targets! Sub-Junior Jeffrey had never broken 100 straight in his target shooting life yet he broke all 200 in the Singles Championship and then outlasted three of the Nation's outstanding singles shooters before he was eliminated and promptly took off to go fishing!"

"Among the high lights of the shoot:"

- "The fresh salmon barbecue provided by the Las Vegas Gun Club members and their families."

- "The free raffles- All shooters were provided free raffle tickets when registering for the shoot at the Club. Drawings were held at the Rio Hotel on Wednesday, Thursday and Friday nights. The prizes were duplicated (and increased) each night and consisted of trays (at least two each night!) containing $100 silver dollars each. The first two nights a trap grade, Remington 1187 shotgun was given away. The third night an SKB trap grade, over and under was the top prize. "There were at least ten items of value given away each night."

"The donors were:"

"Bill Hunter, Las Vegas Gun Club, Rio Hotel, SKB & Guns Unlimited, Grubby's Sportswear, and Remington Arms."

"Dollar Rent A Car and SCOTTSHOT were also sponsors!"

1994 Mid-Winter Tournament- February 22-27

"658 shooters from 39 states and 5 Canadian Provinces made the trip to Las Vegas to participate in the 45th Annual Mid-Winter Trapshooting Tournament. The major attendance by states were; California 150, Nevada 92, Ohio 42, Wisconsin 31, Colorado 28, and Alaska 27. United States shooters came from as far away as Vermont, Hawaii and Alaska."

"The Las Vegas Gun Club and the Rio Suite Hotel hosted the shoot and extended the courtesies that the shooters have come to expect at these shoots. The "no-cost" raffles, featuring trays of 100 silver dollars, shotguns and shooting apparel, that are becoming a prime event at these shoots, were continued with prizes contributed by the Las Vegas Gun Club, The Rio Hotel, and Grubby's Sportswear. Other contributors to the shoot were Scottshot, Dollar-Rent-A-Car and, as ever, Bill Hunter. Bill provided all the Veteran and Senior Veteran Trophies (quarter pound silver ingots) as well as the Lady Runner-Up and Yardage Runner-Up Trophies in the Handicaps. Bill and Larry Scott provided Scottshot for daily winners of a drawing for the shooters in the first ten squads."

"The shooters experienced stiff, cold winds on the first and last day of the shoot. The weather during the rest of the shoot was beautiful."

255

1994 Fall Tournament- September 20-25

"Five hundred and thirty-three shooters, representing 38 States and two Canadian Provinces, fired at over a third of a million targets in attempts to win one, or more, of the sterling silver and gold trophies that the Las Vegas Gun Club offered."

"Excellent weather conditions as well as properly maintained and operated traps resulted in some outstanding scores. There were thirty-seven, 16 yard, 100 straights, eleven, 16 yard 200 straights, three 100 straights in Doubles and eight Handicap 100 straights (seven from the 27 Yard line!) Dan Bonillas broke two of the Doubles straights and one of the Handicap 100s. Young Randy Wilhelm had the other 100 in Doubles and won the High-Over-All. Earl Scripture had a singles long run of 747."

"The Las Vegas Gun Club members put on a delicious fresh salmon barbecue for the shooters and their families. Bill Hunter provided all of the Senior Veteran and Veteran Trophies (engraved sterling silver, silver dollar, money clips each containing a crisp new $20.00 bill). He also contributed all of the Lady and handicap yardage winner runner-up trophies. Bill, Remington Arms, and Keystone Industries provided the trophies for an extra, registered, doubles event (#14). The Las Vegas Gun Club, Rio Suite Hotel and Grubby's Sportswear were the prime movers in putting on three "no charge" raffles where trays of silver dollars, sportswear and a Remington trap gun were won by Fall Tournament shooters. Bill Hunter and Larry Scott contributed SCOTTSHOT to be won by shooters, in the first ten squads, by a daily drawing."

1995 Mid-Winter Tournament- Feb. 28-March 5

"A record number of shooters (for the Las Vegas Gun Club) made the trip to Las Vegas for the annual Mid-Winter Trap Tournament.

787 individual shooters from 44 states and 5 Canadian Provinces made 4335 entries to shoot at 433,500 targets! The major attendance, by states was; California 163, Nevada 86, Ohio 56, Colorado 51, Utah 47, Wisconsin 33, Missouri 28 and Alaska 20. United States shooters came from as far away as Vermont, Alabama and Alaska."

"The Las Vegas Gun Club and the Rio Suite Hotel hosted the shoot and extended all of the courtesies that the shooters have come to expect at these shoots."

"The "no cost" raffles, featuring trays of 100 silver dollars, shotguns and shooting apparel, that has become a prime event at these shoots, were continued with prizes contributed by the Las Vegas Gun Club, The Rio Hotel and Grubby's Sportswear. The Rio Suite Hotel put on a video poker tournament for the ladies, $500 in prize money spiced the competition! Other contributors to the shoot were SCOTTSHOT, Dollar-Rent-A-Car and, as ever, Bill Hunter.

"The shooters encountered a potpourri of weather during this shoot. Every kind of weather from dark, cold, windy days to calm, warm beautiful days were experienced. The shooters didn't seem to mind the weather and the scores were excellent."

1995 Fall Tournament- September 12-17

"Two factors were outstanding at the shoot, hospitality and temperature! The hospitality was supplied by the Rio Suite Hotel and the Las Vegas Gun Club. The temperature was supplied by Mother Nature. The temperature topped out in the triple digits every day until Sunday."

"Four hundred and sixty-six shooter, representing 35 States and two Canadian Provinces, fired at almost a third of a million targets in attempts to win one, or more, of the sterling silver and gold trophies that the Las Vegas Gun Club offered. The trapshoot was the Las Vegas Gun Club's 25th Fall Trapshooting Tournament."

"Hank Lind and the Sahalee Company of Alaska provided fresh silver salmon for an outstanding barbecue for shooters and their families to kick-off the week. Scottshot provided 750 lbs of shot for trophies in a special shoot-off to follow the Scottshot Handicap. Sterling silver and gold trophies were awarded by the club."

"The temperatures topped out in triple digits every day until Sunday, but the humidity remained low."

"Neal Crausbay, after winning the morning handicap with 100-straight, and, despite a moderate Southerly wind, won the final handicap with a lone 99! Larry Bumsted won the High-Over-All by just one target over Bob Munson."

1996 Mid-Winter Tournament- Feb. 27-March 3

"A new Las Vegas Gun Club record number of shooters made the trip to Las Vegas (for many, it was a stormy trip) for the annual Mid-Winter Trap Tournament. 813 individual shooters from 42 States and Canada made the 4273 entries to shoot at 472,300 targets! The major attendance by states was; California 164, Nevada 88, Ohio 77, Colorado 45, Utah 33, Wisconsin 25 Missouri 27, Alaska 24 and Canada 26."

"Early Monday morning, a white mantle of snow covered the Las Vegas Gun Club. From that point on, the weather improved daily until the weekend brought shirt sleeve, almost balmy, weather. The Las Vegas Gun Club and Lady Luck Hotel sponsored a hosted cocktail and hors d'oeuvres cocktail party and raffled off trays of 100 silver dollars and shooting apparel. Dan Bonillas prepared a "hot chicken wing" barbecue for the shooters and their families on Tuesday evening at the club."

"Lancaster, Ohio, shooters "Doc" and Lisa (nee Stuart) Woodward had a good trip and shoot. They were married in Las Vegas and spent their honeymoon trapshooting. Lisa broke 100 straight in the Las Vegas Singles Championship and claimed the Class A title. In the same event, "Doc" broke 25 straight in a shoot-off to earn the Class C Buckle."

"Due to weather delays and large attendance, the 2nd 100 of the Singles Championship was cancelled. There were 11 one hundred straights. **Louie Morgan*** ran another 100 in the shoot-off and won the Champion Buckle."

"Leo Harrison III won the Midwinter Handicap Championship follow 100 straight and a 5-round shoot off over Phil Kiner."

"Prior to the start of the Calcutta on Saturday night, the Las Vegas Gun Club members honored Steve Carmichael's election to the ATA Hall of Fame by presenting him with a very large bottle of liquid "cheer.""

*For some unknown reason, we have no photo to share of Ohio shooter, Louie Morgan. Best known for his handicap prowess, Louie was always a tough competitor.

1996 Fall Tournament- September 24-29

"Nearly 300,000 targets were fired at by 536 contestants representing 36 States and two Canadian Provinces. The tournament was co-hosted by the Las Vegas Gun Club and the Showboat Hotel and Casino."

"Bill Hunter of California provided special medallions at the Showboat's Thursday evening cocktail party, and also donated them to the junior runner-up in three of the handicap events. Highlighting the party were "no cost" raffles, featuring five trays of 100 silver dollars provided by the hotel and the Las Vegas GC, plus a host of other prizes contributed by vendors present at the shoot."

"Just a hint of wind remained Friday morning, and it died completely midway through the feature doubles, making for excellent shooting conditions. Sandra Lewis met Dan Bonillas at the shoot-off stripe to determine the winner of the contest after the two smacked 100 program targets apiece. Dan missed his first bird out but ran the remaining 19, while Sandy let two fly unbroken to earn Class AA laurels."

"Dave McGee earned his ATA 27-yard pin and received his punch from Central Handicap Committee member Gary Sherrod. Tom Buxman won first place in Thursday's $50-50-Bird Handicap with a lone 50 straight from the 27. George Zulkofske paced Saturday's $100 100-Bird Handicap with a lone 99 from 24.5 yards."

"Members of the Las Vegas GC served as chefs for an Alaskan salmon bake Tuesday afternoon, with 200 lbs. of salmon compliments of Hank Lind and Sahalee of Alaska. The host club also provided a free spaghetti dinner on Saturday."

Ron Alcoriza posted the lone 100 straight in Saturday's Winchester Handicap. Bud Rupe defeated Larry Zerngast, Alden Katsutani, Ron Alcoriza, and Dan Watson in shoot-off after posting scores of 99 in the Handicap Championship. High-Over-All winner was Larry Zerngast; 872.

1997 Mid-Winter Tournament- Feb. 25-March 2

"A new Las Vegas Gun Club record number of shooters made the trip to Las Vegas for the annual Mid-Winter Trap Tournament. Eight hundred fifty-four individual shooters from 43 States and Canada made 4376 entries to shoot at 437,600 targets!"

"The shooters encountered a potpourri of weather, everything from icy rain driven by Arctic winds to mild, breezeless, warm days! Some days presented a formidable environment to both shooters and trap personnel! The Las Vegas trap personnel responded to the weather conditions with an excellent performance."

"The Las Vegas Gun Club members prepared a "hot chicken wing" barbecue for the shooters and their families on Tuesday evening at the club. The Showboat Hotel provided a hosted cocktail party, complete with hors d'oeuvres. Almost 700 shooters and family members attended. Trays of 100 silver dollars and a number of prizes provided by the shoot vendors were raffled off. The Club also provided a spaghetti feed on Saturday night."

"The management level of the ATA was well represented at this shoot; Central Handicap Member, Gary Sherrod, won the Lake Mead Singles as well as Champion Runner-Up in the MachOne Midwinter Singles Championship. ATA President, Lucky Nightingale, won the Remington Handicap. ATA Past President Neal Crausbay won the Mid-Winter Doubles Championship, and California Delegate, Kurt Sachau, split the top spot in the $100-100-Bird Handicap. Central Handicap Chairman, Dick Marascola, and Nevada Delegate, Russ McLennan manned the Handicap Desk."

1997 ATA Nevada State Shoot- April 2-6

"The Nevada State Trapshooting Association held their 1997 State Shoot at the Las Vegas Gun Club. The weather progressed from very poor to beautiful at the end!"

"Three hundred seventy-six shooters from 26 States and Canada formed 2103 entries and shot at almost a quarter of a million targets. As usual, the targets were well set and thrown. There was a very minimum of trap problems."

"One of the highlights of the shoot was the "no charge" delicious barbecued halibut dinner furnished to all shooters and their families. The large amount of halibut required was provided by Nevada State Delegate, Russ McLennan. The halibut, and rest of the dinner was prepared by the Las Vegas Gun Club. Russ also donated beautiful buckles to the Junior and Sub-Junior High-All-Around winners. Las Vegas Club member Ron Tseu and the Las Vegas Gun Club put on a unique and delicious shish-kabob barbecue dinner on Friday night. There was no charge for shooters and their families."

1997 Nevada State Champions- (sorry, no photos!)

Singles- Joe Ramos Jr, 200; Out-Of-State- Mike Cunliffe, 200

Doubles- Eli Walker, 99; Out-of-State- Joe Roach, 100

Handicap- Jason Sells, 97; Out-of-State- Steven Eichler, 99

All-Around- Joe Ramos Jr, 392 x 400; Out-of-State- Mike Cunliffe, 391

High-Over-All- Joe Ramos Jr, 763 x 800; Out-of-State- Phil Kiner, 779 x 800

1997 Fall Tournament- September 23-28

"Two factors were outstanding at Las Vegas Gun Club's 27th Fall Trapshooting Tournament, hospitality and scores!"

"Four hundred and ninety-one shooters, representing 35 States and two Canadian Provinces, fired at almost 286,000 targets in attempts to win one, or more, of the sterling silver and gold trophies that the Las Vegas Gun Club offered. The major trophy, at this shoot, was a diamond encrusted, super bowl style ring provided by the MachOne Shotguns for the 16 Yard Champion."

"Among the many highlights of this shoot was the honoring of Amerigo Pagliaroli's retirement after 21 years of shooter service while employed by Remington Arms. The Las Vegas Gun Club presented two huge, decorated sheet cakes to Amerigo, who immediately invited all those present to share in enjoying the cakes."

Remington's Amerigo Pagliaroli celebrates his retirement party at the Las Vegas Gun Club

1998 Mid-Winter Tournament- Feb. 24-March 1

"The 1997-1998 El Nino weather phenomenon not only affected the Nation, it severely impacted shooter participation in the Las Vegas Gun Club's 49th Annual Midwinter Trap tournament. Early in the shoot, the El Cajon Pass, (a major route between Southern California and Las Vegas) was closed by snow. Also, during the shoot, Interstate Highway 99, North of Bakersfield, California, (another major route from Central and Northern California) was closed due to flooding. On the first shoot day, there were over 400 shooters signed in but only slightly more than 100 shooters made it to the traplines. During the first four days, the shooters (and, even more so, the trapline workers) were harassed by rain, sleet, and very cold wind."

"Six hundred sixty-three hardy shooters from 40 States and Canada made 3296 entries and shot at 352,750 targets in competition for beautiful, sterling silver and gold trophies plus a diamond studded, super bowl style, Singles Championship ring!"

"On Tuesday evening at the club, the Las Vegas Gun Club members prepared a hosted fajita carnitas party for the shooters and their families that had many shooters coming back for seconds. The club also provided a spaghetti feed on Saturday night."

"The Rio Suite Hotel put on a benchmark party that will be almost impossible to equal or surpass! The fully hosted party was open to all shooters and their families. Tables were set for 700 people and they were all full! The food went far beyond hors d'oeuvres, it was more than a seven-course dinner."

1998 First North American Handicap Championship-

Apr. 28-May 3

"The Las Vegas Gun Club hosted a very innovative trap shoot. This shoot was designed to offer equal chances of winning major trophies to all trap shooters. The shoot featured not only the usual beautiful sterling silver and gold trophy buckles, it also featured two unusual events; the first, the Vince Bianco shoot-off, offered the shooters a chance to win considerable cash in a 25-round shoot-off. The second special event allowed the shooters to qualify, on a yardage basis, and then shoot-off, again on a 25 by 25 round basis, for a brand, new Chevy pick-up truck, a MachOne trap gun or 18 other valuable trophies!"

"Two hundred eighty-one shooters from 32 States and Canada made up 1653 entries and shot at 152,800 targets in competition for the beautiful sterling silver and gold trophies plus a chance to shoot-off for cash and/or the 1998 Chevy S-10 pick-up truck, the MachOne shotgun and a host of other valuable awards! United States shooters came from as far away as New Hampshire, Alaska, Florida and Hawaii."

The weather was near perfect. The temperatures in the mornings was in the 70s, it climbed into the upper 80s in the afternoons. Those shooters that drove through the Mohave Desert on their way to Las Vegas were treated to a beautiful view of the brief "desert in bloom."

"The Las Vegas Gun Club and Host Hotels (in this case it was the Lady Luck Hotel & Casino) have become famous for the hospitality extended to the shooters and their families. The Lady Luck hosted nightly cocktail parties and raffled off a rack ($100) of dollar tokens. Also, the Lady Luck put on a mini-slot tournament for shooters and their families with the winner guaranteed $500. In addition to an excellent Saturday evening spaghetti dinner furnished by the club, each yardage punch earner was given a half or full yard measuring stick, appropriately inscribed, to remember the event."

"Vince Bianco, a long time, very active member of the Las Vegas Gun Club, retired and moved to Kentucky. Vince, in order to promote trapshooting and to enhance this new shoot, donated $3,000 to be used in a special shoot-off. All of the yardage winners and runner-ups in the first four events were entitled to shoot off for the money. It was divided into four places; 1st- $1200, 2nd- $900, 3rd- $600 and 4th- $300. All of the ties would be shot off, no division of moneys would be allowed."

1st- Daro Handy, 2nd- Kurt Sachau, 3rd- Jimmy Heller, 4th- Ron Zimmerman

Truck winner- Steve Johnson (IL, 25yd) R-U- Ron Zimmerman (NV, 20yd)

1998 Fall Tournament- September 22-27

"Two factors were outstanding at Las Vegas Gun Club's 28th Fall Trapshooting Tournament, hospitality and scores! The hospitality was supplied by the Rio Suite Hotel and the Las Vegas Gun Club."

"Five hundred and forty shooters, representing 33 States, two Canadian Provinces and New Zealand, fired at 332,000 targets in the attempts to win one, or more, of the sterling silver and gold trophies that the Las Vegas Gun Club offered. The major trophy, at this shoot, was a diamond encrusted, super bowl style ring provided by the MachOne Shotgun for the 16-yard Champion. The High-Over-All trophies were Chuck Staple hand-crafted knives. The

266

High-All-Around prizes were beautiful beer steins supplied by Jack and Betty Saik."

"Many people were involved in making this shoot a success. The Las Vegas Gun Club members put on a delicious fresh salmon barbecue for the shooters, and their families. The 200 pounds of fresh silver salmon was a gift from Hank Lind and Sahalee of Alaska company. The Las Vegas Gun Club also provided a free spaghetti dinner on Saturday."

"The weather ranged from good to beautiful! The days started out in the high sixties and never exceeded the very low nineties. The wind varied from none to less than moderate."

The high spot of the shoot was a sumptuous cocktail party and buffet dinner provided by the Rio Suite Hotel. The gala affair was attended by about 600 shooters, their families and friends. Irlene Mandrell was in attendance promoting the 1999 Rio Celebrity Trapshoot the following year to benefit the "Make a Wish" foundation and the ATA Hall of Fame.

Alaska's Evie Seymore was the Handicap Champion with a lone 99, while Ohio's Pat McCarthy won both the High-Over-All and High-All-Around."

1999 Mid-Winter Tournament- Feb. 23-28

"656 Shooters from 36 states, 3 Canadian provinces and New Zealand made the trip to Las Vegas to participate in the celebration of the Golden Anniversary of the Annual Mid-Winter Trapshooting Tournament. The major attendance by states were; California 121, Nevada 77, Ohio and Michigan 37, Colorado 30, Utah 28 and Wisconsin 26. United States shooters came from as far away as Connecticut, Florida, Hawaii and Alaska."

"The Las Vegas Gun Club and the Imperial Palace Hotel hosted the shoot and extended the courtesies that the shooters have come to expect at these shoots."

"The Imperial Palace went all out to celebrate the 50th Anniversary of the Midwinter Tournament! The hotel not only provided "comp" buffet meals for trap shooters who were guests of the hotel, a hosted cocktail party with loaded snack table was also a gift to the guests as well as "no charge" raffle that was held for all the trap shooters. In addition to the prime raffle item of a Beretta 390 trap gun, jackets, sweaters and 3-night, two-day vacation packages were given away."

"The shooters experienced warm weather on Tuesday and Wednesday. Thursday and Friday's shooting was hampered somewhat by windy, cool conditions. Saturday and Sunday were examples of how beautiful Las Vegas can be in the winter. The weather had the trap shooters shedding layers of clothing and looking for a place in the shade."

"The Las Vegas Gun Club highlighted the 50th Anniversary by awarding $50 and a flat of Remington shells to every shooter (no special entry required) that broke a 50-straight in any handicap."

"Phil Kiner led the week's largest event, Saturday's Remington Handicap, with the week's lone perfect century from yardage. He paced the 491-member field by one."

1999 Second North American Handicap Championship

April 27-May 2

"The Las Vegas Gun Club hosted a very innovative trap shoot for the second year. This shoot was designed to offer equal chances of winning major trophies to all trapshooters. The shoot featured not only the usual beautiful sterling and gold trophy buckles, it also featured two unusual events; the first one, the Imperial Palace/Vince Bianco shoot-off, offered the shooters a chance to win considerable cash in a 25-round shoot-off. The second special event allowed the shooters to qualify, on a yardage group basis, to shoot-off for three brand new Chevy Geos, three Browning BT-100 trap guns, three Beretta AL 390 trap guns and a host of other valuable prizes. Dennis DeVault and the MachOne organization donated a $2500 gold coin and silver buckle to be won is a shoot-off of the three car winners."

Three hundred ninety-three shooters from 33 states and Canada made up 2412 entries and shot at 241,200 targets in competition for the beautiful sterling silver and gold trophies plus a chance to shoot off for cash and/or the three 1999 Chevy Geo cars and the host of other valuable awards. United States shooters came from as far away as Connecticut, Alaska, Florida and Hawaii."

"The weather ranged from "not so good" to near perfect. Although torrential rain fell in Las Vegas during the night, the shooters never had to put rain wear on! The rain clouds seemed to split and hug the mountains to the East and West of the club! The temperature in the mornings was in the upper sixties; it climbed to the upper 80s in the afternoons. During most of the afternoons, light winds maintained the apparent temperature in a very comfortable area."

"On Friday and Saturday, a chill Northerly wind kept the shooters in warm clothes. Southerly wind came up a few times and kept the shooters on their toes. On the final day, Sunday, the weather became near perfect until almost time for the shoot-offs! An unusual

Westerly wind and high overcast made the shooting a bit more tricky."

"Many of the nation's top trap shooters were present. Young, 27-yard shooter, Travis Oakey, had an outstanding shoot. He won three 27-yard Winner or Runner-Up Trophies, two Junior awards, the 27-Yard High-Over-All and First place in the Imperial Palace, Bianco Shoot-Off. Texan David McGee broke one of the three 25 straights in the first round of the Car Shoot-offs then went on to break a 50 straight and won the MachOne buckle in the Car Champions' shoot-off! Las Vegas's Ron Stewart and Stockton's Ron Alcoriza won the other two Geos."

"Richard Marshall won the Shoot High-Over-All w/957X1000."

1999 Fall Tournament- September 14-19

"Four hundred and thirty shooters, representing 34 States fired at 272,300 targets in the tournament. The Las Vegas Gun Club's use of voice operated pulling, on all traps, was a major innovation at this shoot. The absence of puller errors drew many favorable shooter comments. This was the first USA use of voice-call equipment in a major shoot. Five handicap 100 straights were broken by 27 Yarders; seventeen 99's were recorded in the handicap events; eleven 200 and 56 100 straights were recorded in the 16 Yard events."

"The shoot featured many presentations. The major item was the presentation to Dick Marascola, ATA Central Handicap Chairman, by the Las Vegas Gun Club and members, of a plaque memorializing the July 22, 1999, Marine Corp ceremony at which Dick was presented with the Nation's third highest military honor, the Silver Star, for actions far beyond the call of duty during the

Korean War. Jimmy Heller's 45th birthday, Tom Buxman's 100,000th 16 Yard target, and Chuck Elton's birthday was also celebrated."

"Las Vegas local Sal Mercadante won the diamond encrusted, super bowl-style ring provided by MachOne for the Single's Championship following 200 and 100 in shoot-off. The Singles Runner-Up was David Van Elgort, also with 200 in the program. The Single's Champion Runner-up trophy, also supplied by MachOne, was a very large sterling silver and gold buckle containing a $25-dollar (face value) gold coin. Larry Bumsted won the Handicap Championship with 100, and Richard Marshall won the High-Over-All with 784."

"Many people were involved in making this shoot a success. The Las Vegas Gun Club members put on a delicious fresh salmon barbecue for the shooters, and their families. The 200 pounds of fresh silver salmon was a gift from Hank Lind and Sahalee of Alaska Company. The Las Vegas Gun Club also provided delicious hors d'oeuvres on Saturday."

2000 Mid-Winter Tournament- Feb. 22-27

"One shoot ends, and another begins- that is the usual course of events on the winter ATA circuit in the desert Southwest. The 51st Mid-Winter Tournament at Las Vegas was scheduled to pick up Monday where the Spring Grand in Phoenix left off Sunday, but forces of nature caused club management to switch to Plan "C" (for cancellation)."

"The crowd already on the grounds had to wait until Tuesday for targets as Monday's 150-pair event, the program's lone twin-bird contest, was scratched due to heavy rain and windstorm. Over 18" of snowfall was recorded on nearby Mt. Charleston."

"In spite of conditions, 619 shooters came from thirty-eight states and three Canadian Provinces and fired at 334,000 targets in their attempts to win silver and gold buckles plus gold coins." Shooters from 38 States and 3 Canadian Provinces made the trip to Las Vegas to participate in the 51st Annual Mid-Winter Trapshooting Tournament. United States shooters came from as far away as Maine, Florida and Alaska."

"The Palace Station was the host hotel and extended the courtesies that the shooters have come to expect at these shoots. The Palace Station put up a gold coin for the guest that scored the highest in the Silver State Handicap (Event 5). Two shooters that traveled together, shot in the same squad, broke the same number of targets; shot off for the coin! Michael Noonan won the coin after a two-round shoot-off with Richard Long."

"Marty Remmes, 21-yarder from New York, captured the first trophy of his career after three extra innings on blustery Thursday, winning Junior Vet over Gordon Mechler and Larry Andorf following scores of 92."

"At the end of the day's handicap, a number between 5 and 15 was drawn at random. The number 12 was selected and subtracted from the top score of 96, with all who broke 84 in the event called to shoot off for a custom-made stock and forend, valued at more than $1,000 and provided by Dennis DeVault of NCP Products. Eight shooters responding to the page fired at 10 birds apiece, with Alaska's Evie Seymore running her targets for the set of wood."

As the Doubles were cancelled to weather, there's no photo for doubles!

2000 3rd North American Handicap Championship

April 25-30

"The weather ranged from near perfect to "not so good". During the first part of the shoot, the temperature in the afternoons was in the mid-nineties with the shooters looking for shade. On Saturday a very cool North wind had everyone putting on extra clothes and looking for a place out of the wind."

"Three hundred thirty-one shooters from 36 States and Canada made up 2076 entries and shot at 207,600 targets in competition for silver and gold trophies plus a chance to shoot-off on a yardage group basis for three new cars, three Browning BT100 trap guns, three Beretta AL390 trap guns and a host of other valuable trophies."

"On Tuesday, the winners of each yardage group, if they had played the car purse, won, in addition to the beautiful sterling silver and gold buckle, two flats of ammo. The Runner-up winners earned one flat of ammo in addition to the buckle."

"The high spot of the day as the complimentary open pit barbecue put on by White Flyer for all of the shooters and their families. The food consisted of delicious chicken and ribs with fresh corn on the cob and all of the fixings."

"Dennis Devault and MACH ONE Guns donated a beautiful custom-made gold coin buckle (valued at $2000) to be the final trophy at this shoot. The three Car Champions shot off to determine the Champion of Champions, the buckle winner and the first pick of car colors. Arizona's Ron Lew won the Buckle and his pick of the cars (he took blue) with a 24. Richard Marshall took the second pick (white) with a 23 while Kyle Fowler was recipient of the remaining car (red) with a 21."

2000 Fall Tournament/ATA Western Satellite Grand- September 18-24; 575 shooters

"Contestants were invited to participate in two separate tournaments; The Las Vegas Fall Tournament ran Monday through Thursday, followed by the ATA Western Satellite Grand Friday, Saturday and Sunday."

"Lent Matthews registered his 100,000th singles target Tuesday. He received the ATA pin from California ATA Delegate Kurt Sachau and a cake from the club."

"Las Vegas Gun Club members hosted a salmon barbecue for shooters and their families Tuesday. The 200 pounds of silver salmon were provided by Hank Lind and Sahalee of Alaska Company. On Wednesday, Dan Bonillas prepared a complimentary chili verde dinner for all those present."

"Bill Hunter donated a silver and gold buckle for the Western Grand All-Around Champion and a silver money clip filled with cash for the runner-up. All-Around awards were 12 steins donated by Jack and Betty Saik. Dave and Patty Grubbs of Grubby's Sportswear provided shirts to all club employees."

"On Friday, Utah Jazz star Karl (the Mailman) Malone and his wife visited the club to try their hand at trapshooting. Karl also spent time at Floyd Lamb State Park helping give fishing lessons to kids. He received pointers on the trap field from Dennis Taylor."

"Former All-American Leah Larkin, daughter of Tom and Vickie, was married to Shad Dixon at 8 p.m. Friday at the Little Church of the West across from Mandalay Bay. Shad is a new ATA shooter, who was attending his first competition. Leah started law school the Monday after the Grand."

Winners during the Western Grand portion of the program as follows- Singles Champion- Dennis Devault, Handicap Champion- Stephen Ollock, Doubles Champion- Harlan Campbell, All-Around

Champion-Sean Hawley, and High-Over-All Champion- Richard Marshall.

2001 Mid-Winter Tournament- Feb. 5 – 11

"Five hundred and seventy-eight individual shooters traveled to Las Vegas and formed 3247 entries. They shot at almost 362,000 targets in attempts to win one or more of the distinctive awards. Shooters from 41 States, 3 Canadian Provinces and England, made the trek to Las Vegas to participate in the 52nd Annual Mid-Winter Trapshooting Tournament. United States shooters came from as far away as Connecticut, Florida, Alaska and Hawaii."

"The shoot program contained several innovations; Class AAA trophies were offered in all of the singles and doubles events. Superbowl-style rings were the top trophies in the Championship events. Silver ingots were the awards in the High-All-Around and the High-Over-All competition. The continued use of voice call pulling met with positive shooter acceptance."

"Many people joined in making the awards for this shoot outstanding. David and Patti Grubbs (Grubby's Sportwear) provided beautifully embroidered shell bags, each complete with four boxes of shells, for all of the Event 7 (Lake Mead Singles) winners. Dennis Devault (MachOne) and Bob Schultz (Bob Schultz target Shotguns) provided a Superbowl-style ring for the Midwinter

Singles Champion, a Gold Coin Belt Buckle for the Champion Runner-Up and $1500 in added money. MACH ONE and Canterbury Voice Release provided a Superbowl-style ring for the Midwinter Doubles Champion. Leigh Edwards and Top Line Porting provided another Superbowl-style ring for the Midwinter Handicap Champion."

"Nigel Chapman, visiting from England, had a very fine week; Nigel won Class A in the Lake Mead Singles, won Champion Runner-Up in the Silver State Handicap, tied for Class AAA in the Class Singles, won Class A in the Doubles Championship, tied for Champion in the Las Vegas Handicap and won Class A in High-Over-All."

"Harlan Campbell won the High-Over-All with 949X1000."

LAS VEGAS GUN CLUB'S GALLERY OF CHAMPIONS

1992-2001

Ron Alcoriza- 1992 Fall Handicap Champion

Bill Anzaldi- 1996 Mid-Winter Doubles Champion

Don Beck- 1997 Fall Handicap Champion

Dan Bonillas- Multiple Venue Winner; Multiple Years

Larry Bumsted- Multiple Venue Winner; Multiple Years

Harlan Campbell- Multiple Venue Winner; Multiple Years

Neal Crausbay- Multiple Venue Winner; Multiple Years

Dean Debow- Multiple Venue Winner; Multiple Years

Edward Halpen Jr.-1997 Mid-Winter Handicap Champion

Daro Handy- Multiple Venue Winner; Multiple Years

Leo Harrison III- Multiple Venue Winner; Multiple Years

Blaine Hartley- 2000 Fall Singles Champion

Terry Harwatt- 2001 Mid-Winter Handicap Champion

Jim Heckroth- Multiple Venue Winner; Multiple Years

Frank Hoppe- 2001 Fall Doubles Champion

Steve Johnson- 1998 NAHC Champion

Phil Kiner- 1997 Fall Singles Champion

Richard Marshall- Multiple Venue Winner; Multiple Years

Paul Matthews- 1998 Mid-Winter Handicap Champion

Mike Mazzucchi- 2001 Mid-Winter Singles Champion

Pete McCall- 1999 Mid-Winter Singles Champion

Pat McCarthy- 1998 Fall HOA Champion

Sal Mercadante- 1999 Fall Singles Champion

Jerald Mitchell- 2000 Mid-Winter Singles Champion

Robert Munson- 1994 Fall Singles Champion

Billy Newton- 1993 Mid-Winter Handicap Champion

Travis Oakey- 2001 Mid-Winter Doubles Champion

Jerry Parr- 1998 Fall Doubles Champion

Cliff Reed- 1993 Fall Singles Champion

Billy Rink- 1999 Fall Handicap Champion

Bud Rupe- 1996 Fall Handicap Champion

Kurt Sachau- 1998 Mid-Winter Handicap Champion

Dan Schock- 1998 Mid-Winter Singles Champion

Ron Schroer- 1995 Fall Singles Champion

Earl Scripture/Ross Warren- 1993 Fall Singles Co-Champions

Evie Seymore- 1998 Fall Handicap Champion

Dave Siegler- 2001 Fall Handicap Champion

Ray Stafford- Multiple Venue Winner; Multiple Years

Carl Swanson- 1994 Mid-Winter Singles Champion

Randy Wilhelm- 1994 Fall HOA Champion

Sonny Young- 1992 Fall Singles Champion

David Zanotti- Multiple Venue Winner; Multiple Years

Larry Zerngast- 1996 Fall HOA Champion

Ron Zimmerman- 1998 NAHC Champion Runner-Up

Group Photo- 1999 North American Handicap Championship

from left to right-

Steve Carmichael- LVGC Host

Dave McGee- NAHC Champion & Mid-Yardage Car Winner

Ron Stewart- NAHC Short-Yardage Car Winner

Ron Acoriza- NAHC Long-Yardage Car Winner

Dennis DeVault- NAHC Sponsor of the Champions Buckle

Ron Lew- 2000 N.A.H.C. Champion

Champions Photos

Ron Alcoriza, CA

Bill Anzaldi, MA

Don Beck, TX

Dan Bonillas, CA

Champions Photos (cont.)

Larry Bumsted, IA

Harlan Campbell, KS

Neal Crausbay, TX

Dean Debow, KY

Edward Halpen Jr, RI

Daro Handy, OR

Leo Harrison III, MO

Blaine Hartley, UT

Champions Photos (cont.)

Terry Harwatt, WV

Jim Heckroth, NV

Frank Hoppe, NE

Steve Johnson, IL

Champions Photos (cont.)

Phil Kiner, WY

Richard Marshall, NE

Paul Matthews, CA

Mike Mazzucchi, CA

Champions Photos (cont.)

Pete MCall, KY

Pat McCarthy, OH

Sal Mercadante, NV

Jerald Mitchell, AZ

Champions Photos (cont.)

Robert Munson, MN

Billy Newton, KS

Travis Oakey, UT

Jerry Parr, CA

Champions Photos (cont.)

Cliff Reed, NE

Billy Rink, KS

Bud Rupe, AZ

Kurt Sachau, CA

Champions Photos (cont.)

Dan Schock, OH

Ron Schroer, AZ

Earl Scripture, TX
Ross Warren, OH

Evie Seymore, AK

Champions Photos (cont.)

Dave Siegler, NV

Ray Stafford, CO

Carl Swanson, CO

Randy Wilhelm, OH

Champions Photos (cont.)

Sonny Young, CO

David Zanotti, CA

Larry Zerngast, KS

Ron Zimmerman, NV

Champions Photos (cont.)

A pick-up truck and six automobiles were given away as prizes at the Las Vegas Gun Club in 1998, 1999 & 2000
These are believed to be the last vehicles provided as awards for a trapshooting competition

Ron Lew, Arizona
The last N.A.H.C. Champion in 2000